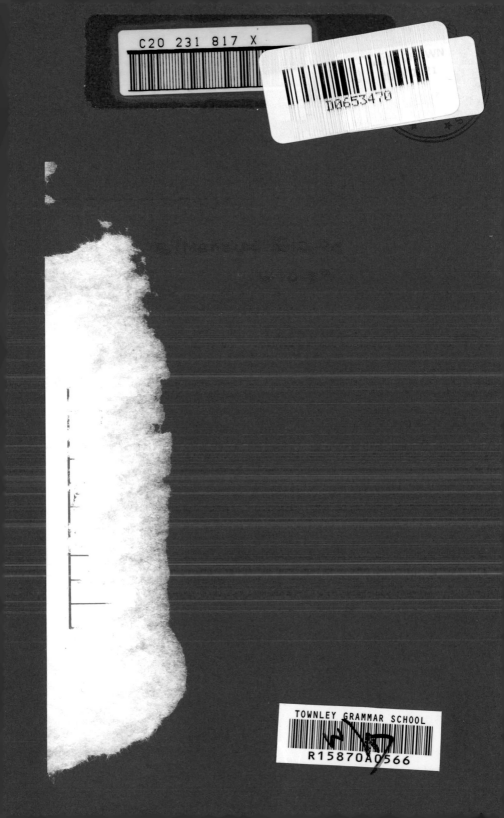

Robert De Niro

Robert De Niro

The Man, the Myth and the Movies

PATRICK AGAN

ROBERT HALE · LONDON

© *Patrick Agan 1989*
First published in Great Britain 1989

Robert Hale Limited
Clerkenwell House
Clerkenwell Green
London EC1R 0HT

British Library Cataloguing in Publication Data

Agan, Patrick 1943–
    Robert De Niro : the man, the myth, and the movies.
    1. American cinema films. Acting. De Niro, Robert.
    Biographies
    I. title   72|8⁹
    791.43′028′0924

ISBN 0–7090–3763–5

Set in Palatino by
Derek Doyle & Associates, Mold, Clwyd.
Printed in Great Britain by
St Edmundsbury Press Ltd, Bury St Edmunds, Suffolk.
Bound by WBC Bookbinders Limited.

Contents

Illustrations

Acknowledgements

The author wishes to thank many informants, publications and friends for their varied and vital contribution to this book: Hank Grant, Robert Osborne and Martin E. Grove of *The Hollywood Reporter*, Liz Smith, *The New York Daily News*, Chris Chase, *Observer* magazine, *Sight and Sound*, Janet Charlton, Stephen Farber, Marie Brenner, *The Movie Brats* by Michael Pye and Lynda Miles, *Life* magazine, Earl Blackwell's Celebrity Register, Peter Rainer of the *Los Angeles Herald-Examiner*, *TV Guide*, Barbara Goldsmith, *The Sun*, *People* magazine, Wolfgang Wilke, *Rolling Stone* magazine, *The Los Angeles Times*, Douglas Heay, *The Daily Mail*, *American Film*, *New York* magazine, *Wired* by Bob Woodward, *The New York Post*, Cindy Adams, *The Daily Express*, Patricia Bosworth, *The Cinema of Robert De Niro* by James Cameron-Wilson, *Robert De Niro, The Hero Behind the Masks* by Keith McKay and Doug McClelland and The Doug McClelland Collection. Special thanks to Gerrold Turnbull and to the staff of the Margaret Herrick Library of the Academy of Motion Picture Arts and Sciences.

To three beautiful women:
Jorn Horn, a matchless English rose
Lisa Rich, a hardy New England wildflower
the late Joyce Jameson, a lush California hybrid

A Day at the Top – De Niro-Style

Paramount Pictures was under siege. The studio's fabled arched entrance off Hollywood's Melrose Avenue was ringed with extra security on the crisp morning of 30 January 1987, and raw excitement was in the air.

Paparazzi mingled with the extra police while inside the gates the usually star-sated studio personnel were gathered at open windows to cheer on the seemingly endless parade of celebrities being chauffered by. The studio was celebrating its seventy-fifth anniversary, and to commemorate the event they were bringing together their most glamorous and legendary attractions for the ultimate Paramount party.

It seemed to onlookers that every limousine in town had been booked for this occasion as a steady stream of them moved under the white arches and down the studio's streets, each carrying a particular piece of Paramount's history. Veterans such as Gregory Peck, Jane Russell, Jimmy Stewart, Olivia de Havilland, Burt Lancaster, Bob Hope and Don Ameche alighted to mingle with the latest star hierarchy represented by the likes of Matthew Broderick, Timothy Hutton and wife Debra Winger, Marlee Matlin, Jennifer Beals and Kevin Costner. For many of them, the past and the future were meeting for the first time.

In all there were over three dozen stars present, representing the studio's top box-office films, from *Samson and Delilah* (Victor Mature) to *Top Gun* (Tom Cruise).

Amidst all the activity, there was one face seldom seem in public: Robert De Niro.

To watch him warily make his way through the notables, clad in casual dark jacket and black-and-white checked shirt, one

11

might easily think he was a studio underling hoping for a close-up look at the action, but the respect with which he was greeted made it clear he was among his own. After all, it was Paramount Pictures who had presented him in his first major commercial film, *The Godfather Part II*, a movie that had added its own megamillions to the studio's Hall of Fame. Since that 1974 triumph, he'd carefully manufactured the image of a reclusive actor, a star who appeared in public only when *he* wanted to.

Life magazine was there to cover Paramount's party, and De Niro quickly became one of their prime targets. He didn't disappoint them either as he mixed and quietly mingled with old friends and older legends. When chatting with Hope, Stewart, de Havilland and company, he showed the respectful demeanour he'd cultivated for his role as a studio leader in *The Last Tycoon*, courteous and diplomatic. Towards his friends and peers, including the ageless Elizabeth Taylor, he was courtly and quiet, amiable yet a bit distant. In short, he was being himself.

When *Life* had distilled its dozens of shots of that day, the importance of his presence was underscored when their special issue came out – with De Niro cover-centre, surrounded by Harrison Ford, Molly Ringwald, Tom Cruise, Faye Dunaway and Mr and Mrs Hutton, with the caption 'The Stars Celebrate Hollywood.' That Hollywood, so different from the one he'd imagined as a kid on New York's Lower East Side who haunted the local cinemas, had now obviously taken him to its heart – and exactly on the terms he wanted.

Introduction

When director Brian De Palma was asked to describe his friend Robert De Niro in one word, he didn't waste much time mulling it over. 'Chameleon,' he said quickly, because, 'He has the uncanny ability to literally change himself into the character he's playing. It's not the trait of a "movie star", someone who builds and perpetuates one specific screen image and then plays variations on that same theme for years, but rather the habit of a man who is truly an *actor*.'

And a very popular one, as proven when shortly after that interview De Palma's *The Untouchables* opened to both critical and popular delight, with many reviews overlooking leading man Kevin Costner and centring instead on De Niro's chillingly grandiose portrayal of mobster Al Capone. Once again the actor had submerged the man, and the result was yet another, newer shade of the chameleon.

Ironically it was playing a gangster in *Mean Streets* some fourteen years before that had first brought De Niro into prominence and yet another, as the young Vito Corleone in *The Godfather Part II*, that solidified his appeal. The pre-release 'buzz' – Hollywood's inside gossip grapevine – on *Godfather II* predicted a huge success, and De Niro's subsequent acclaim, not to mention the Oscar he'd shortly win for the part, quickly made him a major film presence, one of the few personalities whose name alone could get a movie financed and into production.

And no matter how wildly different each role might be – and they've ranged from *Taxi Driver*'s homicidal Travis Bickle to a Catholic priest in *True Confessions* – his name also guarantees the allure of professional perfection. Like seeing a streetwise Laurence Olivier, one can go to any film he stars in and be assured of seeing dynamic acting no matter what the part calls for. And, as with Olivier, the comparison must be drawn with his exceptional ability to find, expand, improvise and help create the character that ends up on screen.

Hollywood is known as being a town built on gossip, innuendo, rumour and, finally, the facts behind all the aforementioned. This talk – the buzz – can mean a lot towards the making or breaking of films and the careers of their stars. Long gone are the days of the old studio system when an actor was signed to a long-term contract and then carefully showcased in pictures designed to build him or her to stardom. When Bobby De Niro came to town, that system was just a memory, and a fresh new face had only one or two chances at gaining the public's attention before being marked for quick oblivion. De Niro has defied that rule to make some of his own, and they've mostly all worked, due largely to his persistent habit of losing himself in his craft.

Paul Schrader, the man who created the *Taxi Driver* and then cemented his talents with *American Gigolo*, once said that De Niro just '...doesn't feel the need to establish an identity apart from his screen persona. He doesn't want to. The only thing he desires to be public about himself is his work. That's the only thing he estimates has any real value.' Schrader is probably right, as it has been De Niro's work that speaks the most loudly about both the actor and the man behind it. Also he did it very much against the odds for, as a leading man, he was an unlikely candidate.

Male superstars before him, like Redford, Newman and Robert Wagner, and the up-and-coming Brat Packers, like Rob Lowe, had all relied on a Look and a Personality to see them through film after film, whereas De Niro falls into the special category of a star actor who's often barely recognizable from one part to the next. Like his true peers, Dustin Hoffman, Al Pacino and Mickey Rourke, he's not only able but also very willing to submerge his own personality to find the heart of a character, often adopting his looks, mannerisms and physical characteristics for as long as necessary to do his job.

This devotion to his craft has often been no little physical challenge. For the role of Jake La Motta in *Raging Bull*, for example, he was not just a star name taking a crack at a famous person *à la* James Cagney in *Yankee Doodle Dandy*, or, from the sublime to the ridiculous, George Hamilton trying to be country music star Hank Williams. Instead he chose to *become* the older La Motta by gorging himself for weeks on Italian food until he'd packed sixty pounds on his slender frame. 'I could have used padding and makeup,' he said later, 'but that would have taken hours to put on every day ... and you never get it quite right around the neck.'

'Getting it right' is his motto – despite personal costs secured along the way. He suffered severe stomach cramps while both gaining and then losing those sixty pounds but even that helped him realize the plight of overweight people in a very personal way.

During the shooting of the later scenes of *Raging Bull* – when De Niro/La Motta was at his heaviest – his stepdaughter expressed her dismay at him. 'She didn't exactly tell me to stop picking her up at school but she was embarrassed by my fat and the fact that I'd thinned out the front of my hair to duplicate Jake's baldness.'

On the brighter side, he also learned women's attitudes towards big men. 'Well, you know the men anyway make out OK. There is a type of woman that is attracted to those chunky teddy-bear men. They really go for it. That was an interesting thing to learn ... and they never recognized it was me!'

A Method actor from his teenager years on, De Niro builds a character from the ground up, living in its skin to make it believable first to himself and then to the audience. This sense of investing life into make-believe has been a defence-mechanism of his for most of his life.

As the son of an Irish-Italian father and a Jewish mother and raised in 'little Italy', he remained at arm's length from both cultures, preferring instead to try to blend into the artistic lifestyle of his highly talented and equally temperamental parents. He was a Method actor, in fact, long before he knew that approach to life even had a name! As an artist, he's used his own flesh and blood to treat himself like a piece of living sculpture in search of simple truths – and he's made that truth surface through virtually every portrait in a now striking gallery of characters. Yet the hardest person to find in all these various guises is De Niro himself.

Stardom equates to money, and money to power: a rule he's adopted for himself with relentless enthusiasm. His life is peopled with carefully chosen friends and business associates, steadily weaving a curtain of privacy around himself which is pierced only by himself and only when he deems it necessary. In fact, he's gradually become so private that in 1981 he was actually detained at Rome's major airport as a suspected terrorist because of his failure to identify himself properly. And this came just after he had won his Oscar for *Raging Bull*!

To De Niro, stardom is simply a means to an end – being able to select the best projects in which to inject his awesome energy and to keep his life as quietly private as possible. A clue to his outlook on Hollywood in general came after the release of *The King of Comedy*, in which he played the obsessed Rupert Pupkin who's willing to trade his bleak future for one brief moment of television glory. The film was a dark and gloomy look at the squirmy underbelly of fame and those attracted to it. When he was asked about its cynical view, De Niro's answer reflected the fact that he personally suffered from as few delusions about stardom and its many edges as he did about life in general. 'If it is bleak, that is because I see show business that way.' Obviously this is not a man with stars in his eyes.

De Niro is a self-constructed enigma who now commands great respect. Instead of being a pre-packaged star as in the old studio contract days, he's seen fit to manufacture himself – and to be able to change that self into any shape or characterization that might be required. And he's obviously done very well with it, especially in the money department. Since the enormous success of *The Untouchables*, his price per picture has skyrocketed to $5 million, and there have been several takers.

People, especially frustrated interviewers, have called him a male Garbo; remote and distant because there's nothing there all that interesting. An easy out, but not the case. As a child, he isolated himself from acceptance, turning instead to a world of make-believe. Now, as an adult, famous the world over, he's at liberty to forge his own identity just exactly as he likes. Startling in his talent, it's been the mainstay of his life and the one thing that has seen him through its many twists and turns.

1   *Opening Act*

During the war years of 1941–5, New York was the 'open city' of the world. Pulsing with the energy of the war effort and the refugees from Hitler's insane outrages, it was an intellectual, political and artistic boiling-pot for the brave and daring minds who had found it a sanctuary from an uneasy world.

The French superliner *Normandie*, sunk by terrorists at her berth in New York harbour, seemed a symbol of the isolation of the United States from the rest of the beleaguered world. Of necessity, the city flourished, and Greenwich Village became the 'bohemian' centre. With Paris occupied by the Nazis, the Village became by default the artistic capital of the world, a magnet for disenfranchized talent from around the world and for Americans as well.

Robert De Niro Senior was one of those up-and-coming – and struggling – artists of that open era. Half Italian, half Irish, the handsome youth, with his shock of romantically dark curls, had nurtured his artistic talents in his home town of Syracuse, New York state, and had moved to the Village to explore and expand them. It was a period of artistic explosion, and De Niro Sr was in the vanguard, interpreting the changes via his own avenue of Abstract Expressionism.

He had studied under Hans Hoffmann in Provincetown, Rhode Island, and while there was attracted to another young artist, Virginia Admiral, an Oregon-born intellectual and a woman much ahead of her time, her streak of independence broad and strong. When they continued their studies with Hoffmann at his West 8th Street studio in New York, they grew steadily closer until finally deciding to marry. Both young and bursting with energy and talent, their personalities were still artistically cantankerous on occasion but together they put on a united and happy front.

In the early 1940s, before their son was born, the couple began bringing together their fellow artists and friends every week or so in a loosely structured 'salon' at their second-floor apartment on Bleecker Street. These friends were also enjoying early successes and working through early defeats, and the De Niros' get-togethers were important to them. The couple couldn't afford much in the way of food or liquor, but who noticed when the talk was good and the companionship even better? Their hostess was the spark that usually set off the festivities. Artist Nell Blaine recalled that, 'Virginia was the only student I knew at that time to sell a painting to the Museum of Modern Art', which fact added a touch of glamour to the simply furnished but brightly art-filled apartment. 'Virginia and De Niro were considered among the most talented, the most gifted, of Hoffmann's students. We talked about them with great respect. They left an aura at the school, where people were either "geniuses" or nothing.' And they were both exhibited first at Peggy Guggenheim's gallery, alongside Jackson Pollack and Mark Rothko.

These optimistic achievements opened up to the couple much of the New York art world, many of whose members dropped by their salon. The De Niros were unconsciously emulating the casual manner of Paris in the twenties, and both were flush with the budding promise of their careers and their choice of stimulating friends. On any given Sunday, one might run into poet Robert Duncan in spirited conversation with artist Marjorie McKee, critic Clement Greenberg or any of the sharpest writers from the *Partisan Review*. Film essayist Manny Farber might be chatting over coffee with Hans Hoffmann himself in an interesting intermingling of creative spirits. Said Nell Blaine, 'Our standards were so pure, we treated with scorn any humdrum references to the personal.' It was lively and occasionally volatile, with the usual underpinnings of social insularity common to any band of individualists.

And for a time it seemed the De Niros were leading a charmed life, capped off on 17 August 1943 when their only child, Robert Junior, was born. He was a miniature version of his father in looks, while emotionally he was a mixture of Irish, Italian and Jewish heritages – a combustible mixture, to say the least.

Unfortunately there were other forces now at work in the lives of the young parents. 1943 marked a time when psychoanalysis was erupting, complete with accented gurus popping out from beneath every couch. Spouting early psycho-babble, they found impressionable artists particularly easy targets for their theories, and the De Niros were no exception.

A friend of the couple described the scene to the *Observer*'s Paul Gardner in 1977, saying, 'Many artists who knew Hans Hoffmann went to a particular shrink whose patients (eventually) had terrible crises and breakdowns. But he couldn't help them. He was a frustrated man – a failed artist, who meddled.' Call it meddling or self-discovery or whatever you want to, but it didn't help the De Niros. In fact, once the dust had settled on this hurricane of new ideas about relationships, ideals and desires, the couple decided they weren't right for each other and, in the spring of 1946, they split up.

Virginia moved with her two-year-old son to a small block of flats on West 14th Street, giving up her art to begin a typing and offset-printing service to support them. Shortly afterwards she became involved with Manny Farber, and he moved in too. It was years before she would paint seriously again. (Years later, at a Hollywood party, Farber approached De Niro, asking, 'Do you remember me? I used to go out with your mother.' According to other guests, Bobby couldn't get out of there fast enough.)

In the battle of art versus survival, Virginia chose the latter – and never looked back. When recently asked about those days, she withdrew quickly, saying, 'I want to keep my life *my* life.'

While the break-up and subsequent divorce were amicable, there's little evidence that De Niro Sr had much to do with raising his son. His main talent for handling the world at large – 'he makes friends easily' – was one obviously lost on young Bobby.

A family friend told writer Patricia Bosworth that the little boy was 'never coddled'. Instead he quietly became his own best friend and given to an increasing shyness and long silences.

Enrolled at Public School 41 in the Village, the youngster proved to be neither an impressive nor much impressed student. His favourite activity seemed to be observing others, and that became the lifelong habit that later would help him greatly when it came time to seek out his own niche in life. Bobby loved wandering around the busy, colourful streets of the Village and nearby Little Italy, checking out the small and seedy bars, poolhalls and bowling-alleys.

Thin, pale and woefully shy, he tried making friends by joining a street gang headquartered on Kenmare Street, a rough-and-tumble group of kids who banded together more for companionship than grabbing territory. For the first time he found himself accepted for being exactly what he was – and took their nickname for him, 'Bobby Milk', because it fitted. Often, before he'd made friends, he would stand across the street from a group of kids and just watch, too shy to join them. 'Bobby Milk' suited him 'because he was pale and strange as milk', a friend recalled.

But other influences were creeping into his life as well. When Robert Sr took his son to the movies, it was the beginning of a lifelong affair between the boy and the silver screen. Since their divorce, De Niro Sr and Virginia had remained respectful friends, and there was never any problem about Bobby's spending time with his father. Also, with a third person in the small apartment, Bobby enjoyed spending time away from it. Ironically one of his favourite movie haunts was Variety Photoplay in the East Village, a place that would figure prominently later in *Taxi Driver* in his scenes with Jodie Foster.

Back at PS 41, at the age of ten, he took a giant step in his life when he appeared in a school play, a production of *The Wizard of Oz*. Appropriately enough he was picked to play the shyest character in the story, the Cowardly Lion who is desperately searching for the courage to make himself whole. At the climax of the piece young Bobby was given the Lion's Medal of Valour as a symbol of the creature's new-found inner strength and, almost as the prop decoration was pinned to his costume, he made a decision: he knew that he wanted to have the make-believe of acting as a permanent part of his life because, finally, 'I could express myself.'

And the irony of his part as the lion isn't to be lost, since, astrologically, he was one already. His birthdate of 17 August puts him squarely under the sign of Leo, which is symbolized by a lion, and with a lion's courage once he'd made his mind up, he set out to make his dreams work.

Once fastened on acting as a possible life's work, Bobby ran into little resistance from his parents. His mother had once noted that, 'His idea of school was just not to show up.' Also, despite his apparent lack of interest in studying, as artists themselves his parents revelled in free expression and experimentation and so actively encouraged him in his new ambition.

Soon Bobby became a movie freak and, since his mother didn't object, began spending as many hours as possible in the rundown cinemas that dotted the neighbourhoods of lower Manhattan. His formal education may have suffered through lack of regular attendance but his knowledge of the movies and their stars gave him a crash course in screen acting.

And happily it was a time of great movies. He saw them all, and in doing so witnessed the screen explosions of the top new actors of the time, including Montgomery Clift, Marlon Brando and, a bit later, James Dean. These screen rebels undoubtedly struck a sympathetic chord in the stringy youngster barely into his teens, and he identified with their roles of isolation, frustration and misunderstanding. Seeing the tortured Clift in *A Place in the Sun* or Brando in either *A Streetcar Named Desire* or *On the Waterfront* must have made for spellbinding afternoons, the kind that set a young mind spinning into all sorts of fantasies and possibilities.

Yet De Niro was nothing if not a budding realist, and while he might appreciate watching Jimmy Dean torturously mumble his way through *Rebel Without a Cause* and *East of Eden*, he never thought it would be easy to do himself, this being an actor. His parents had taught him that artistic acceptability came only after long and painful work during which you dissect yourself and then remake your emotions into the ones suitable to bringing a written part to full-blown life. He knew more and more that he wanted to do it, but he didn't know how.

At the age of sixteen he decided to try to find out, when he quit high school to pursue acting in earnest. Even at that young age, he realized that *now* was the time to start and that regular schooling couldn't offer it. Later he said that his high school years, what few there were, had been '...a bad scene. I was at Rhodes. I went to Music and Art. One semester.' He wanted to tackle the world at large and the world of acting because it always seemed to offer more than what he already had.

During the 1950s New York City acting schools and ideologies abounded – and Bobby promptly proceeded to bound into several of the brightest ones, starting off at the Dramatic Workshop. As his personally assigned homework, he'd buy, read and keep every book available on acting and its diverse

theories. He also attended the Luther James Studio and made
his first bit of money as an actor when he appeared in a
production of Chekov's *The Bear*, which toured local schools. He
loved the experience, and many of his friends thought it was like
Lancelot finding the Holy Grail, he was that serious. A friend
recalled that, 'You never saw Bobby, even at that age, when he
didn't have a paperback book or something under his arm.
You'd go to his house on 14th Street and there'd be a zillion hats
around, all kinds of costumes.'

One casting director, Marion Dougherty, told writer Marie
Brenner that she'd never forget the first time he came in to meet
her: 'He had a portfolio in which he appeared as an
eighty-year-old man, and in costumes of all kinds. I had never
seen anything like that.'

By then he'd begun studying with one of the leaders of the
Method School, Stella Adler, and, knowingly or not, was already
a disciple of her basic tenet, 'Your talent lies in your choice.'
He'd been making choices all his life, the most important being
to restructure his personality, complete with its warts of shyness
and silence, to make it all work for him as an actor.

His parents' separation and divorce, the subsequent change
in lifestyle plus the combination of three strong heritages all
helped form his unique persona. Stella Adler's scene study
classes, which he began in 1960, helped him to use all this input
in a positive way. Her ability to help a young actor to find a
character, build its background and then positively analyse it,
has been a cornerstone of both his talent and career. Now he
was learning to take even the most painful experiences of his life
and make them a positive influence. His ability to get inside a
character – sometimes at great expense to his own body, not to
mention the patience of his co-workers – has since become
legendary.

Later he studied with Lee Strasberg at the Actors' Studio,
taking Strasberg's quiet instructions in the very halls where
Clift, Brando and Dean had also studied. Strasberg was a genius
and quickly recognized the enormity of De Niro's gift, and he
willingly offered him hints and signs to follow on the road to
being a true actor.

In 1975 De Niro attempted to make *Time* magazine
understand why he'd gone to such diverse lengths to polish his
craft to a shining edge. 'At first, being a star was a big part of it.

When I got into it, it became more complicated. To totally submerge into another character and experience life through him without having to risk the real-life consequences – well, it's a cheap way to do things you would never dare to do yourself.'

During those lean beginning years, which stretched through most of the sixties, there weren't many roles that Bobby didn't dare to tackle just as long as he could get on stage and act. He took parts in literally anything he could, and the assortment of roles was catholic at best, including such off-beat items as the German Expressionist play *Cry in the Streets*. Along more American classic lines, he happily worked in 'dinner theatres' when the opportunity came up. 'You had to wait on tables also – but I thought it was a good experience. A lot of actors said it was beneath them, but I made enough in tips to live without worrying when I wasn't working.' These productions included *Cyrano de Bergerac*, *Compulsion* and *Long Day's Journey Into Night*. Yet he was also ready when the unexpected came along, as it did in 1968 when he was cast to play several different characters in the Off-Off-Broadway frolic *Glamour, Glory and Gold*.

When Bobby had first dropped out of high school in 1959, the Off-Broadway arena of theatre had already become a respected venue. Seven years before, Geraldine Page had almost singlehandedly legitimized it with her star-making performance in Tennessee Williams' *Summer and Smoke*. The languid drama had been an enormous hit at the Circle in the Square Theatre in the heart of Greenwich Village, and along with its acclaim came respectability as well for the small theatres and ambitious productions then springing up all over the area. Suddenly Off-Broadway wasn't such a bad place to be, especially when its reputation was further upgraded by hits such as 1954's *The Threepenny Opera*, *The Golden Apple* and a revival of *The Seagull*.

Off-*Off*-Broadway was a natural extension which spread to tiny theatres throughout downtown Manhattan, providing ample space for actors, writers and directors to try their wings in often bizarre productions, of which *Glamour, Glory and Gold* was certainly one. Written by Jackie Curtis, it was the saga of 'Nola Noonan', an ambitious actress from Chicago who wins Hollywood fame only to lose it in a sea of booze. The star was the late Candy Darling, a transvestite 'superstar' discovered and promoted by Andy Warhol (as was author Curtis), and she had an awesomely good time playing the movie star on the way up, over and out. Though technically a man, Candy was a woman in every other sense of the word. This author recalls talking to her and Rex Reed one night at photographer Francesco Scavullo's Eastside townhouse where he was throwing a 'high school graduation' party for her. Emulating her idol, Marilyn Monroe, Candy whispered her excitement over the affair with unabashed appreciation. 'I never had a graduation party,' she purred in her best Marilyn voice as she greeted everyone there, from Halston to any of the other 'underground' stars present in her honour.

Her friend Curtis had written this Hollywood soap opera for Candy (after her death it was revived with Curtis as star), and it was a typically outrageous piece of sixties camp nonsense which allowed her to do her Marilyn Monroe imitation and her co-star, Bobby, to act out the various parts of her husbands, boyfriends and leading men. It was not a hit but it served its purpose as Candy got good reviews – making her a star in her own mind – while Bobby's were better. The *Village Voice* enthused that he'd been able to make '…distinct character statements in a series of parts which many actors would have fused into a general mush. De Niro is new on the scene and deserves to be welcomed.'

At the time Bobby was dating actress Sally Kirkland's room-mate. Kirkland, a recent Oscar nominee for *Anna*, was just starting out herself and, after hearing how terrific this new actor was, journeyed downtown to Bastiano's Cellar Studio to check him out. She was amazed at what she saw, for the man on stage was a far cry from the 'sweet' guy who'd occasionally been knocking on her front door with a fistful of flowers for her room-mate. This man was a genius.

'He played five parts,' she told Marie Brenner. 'I'd never seen anything so brilliant. I went backstage and told him "Do you know that you are going to be the most incredible star?" ' De Niro could barely mumble an acknowledgement. 'He was unbelievably shy. I thought perhaps I was embarrassing him. But I could tell that, more than anything, he wanted to believe it.'

Further proof of his need for affirmation came almost immediately, when he began phoning her instead of the room-mate, always asking, 'Do you really think I'm any good? Do you really?'

Though struggling for her own identity as an actor at that time, Sally Kirkland nonetheless did all she could to encourage her new friend. Slender, blonde and gorgeous, she was quick to appreciate the young actor's sexuality, even though he often took pains to disguise his looks. She was also witness to the breadth of his fertile imagination. At the Actors' Studio they worked together developing various scenes from plays for the Playwright/Directors Unit, spending long hours rehearsing at his 14th Street flat. 'We had so much rage and energy in us,' she later told Patricia Bosworth. 'We would go at each other, have knockdown fights – kitchen-sink-drama-style.'

Just off that small kitchen was Bobby's workshop, the place where he'd spend endless hours working out his characterizations. 'Bobby had this walk-in closet. It was like going into a costume room backstage of a theatre. He had every conceivable kind of getup imaginable – and the hats! Derbies, straw hats, caps, homburgs. And Bobby had this composite he'd carry around with him to auditions – twenty-five pictures of himself in various disguises. In one he was like an IBM executive, in another a professor with glasses and a goatee [shades of his future *Angel Heart* portrayal?], in another a cabdriver – to prove to casting directors he wasn't an exotic. And he'd always have a stack of paperback novels with him too – ideas for characters he might play, might turn into screenplays for himself. He was totally focused on his work.'

One evening Sally had a private dinner with Bobby's mother, Virginia, and during it she seized the opportunity to find out more about Bobby, particularly the secret of his ambitions for success. Virginia paused, thought about it and then answered, '*Will. Force of will.*'

After sharing countless hours of hoping, dreaming and working, De Niro reached a point where he felt comfortable offering Sally some advice. After an audition, he offered both guidance and a speck of personal insight when he told her, 'You are giving away too much. Hold something back. Be mysterious. It's more seductive.' All these tips were ones he'd work into his own acting personality.

Sally Kirkland was a good friend, one of the first people to take up Bobby's cause and happily introduced him to others who might do the same, notably her friend Shelley Winters. And *that* was a meeting of the minds. Sally took Shelley down to see him perform, and the actress was much impressed. Their introduction in an Eighth Avenue bar called Jimmy Ray's was the beginning of a long personal and professional relationship. Later she remembered her first impression: 'Bobby was skinny with very gentle, dark watchful eyes. He didn't say much. He had very little money and he rode around town on a rickety bike.' Shelley recognized the specialness of Bobby's talent and personality, and when the time was right to begin putting together the movie *Bloody Mama*, she remembered him instantly.

2 The Big Screen Beckons

Shelley Winters wasn't the only one to express interest in Bobby during the sixties. Another person was budding film-maker Brian De Palma, who in 1964 was putting together his first feature film, *The Wedding Party*. De Palma had already made a bit of a name for himself with a silent comedy short called *Wotun's Wake*, the third film he'd made while still a student at New York's Columbia University. While widely praised and awarded, the film wasn't a financial success, and De Palma in his way was learning his craft by the seat of his pants – the way Bobby was learning about acting. Brian was learning his film grammar by making films – often both the easiest and most difficult way to learn anything.

At this point, though, he had raised the necessary $100,000 from a friend he knew from Sarah Lawrence College, where he'd been awarded an MCA writing fellowship. His friend, Cynthia Moore, who used the name Cynthia Munroe, not only was the backer of the project but served as well as co-director, co-producer, co-writer *and* co-editor with De Palma and Wilford Leach, a teacher at the university.

It was a shot-in-the-dark move and would prove to be a learning experience that would stretch over several years but De Palma grabbed it. At one of his first open casting calls (where everyone who shows up is seen) he found a young actress named Jill Clayburgh whom he quickly signed to play the bride. Shortly after, he signed on more newcomers: Jennifer Salt, daughter of Waldo Salt, the once-blacklisted writer, Jared Martin, who years later climbed to fame as a regular on television's *Dallas*, and Robert De Niro.

De Palma was initially unimpressed with the young actor but quickly came to change his mind. He was '...very mild, shy, self-effacing. He asked if he could do a scene from acting class.

27

He disappeared for fifteen minutes and returned doing a heavy Lee J. Cobb number.' The shyness disappeared when Bobby '...burst into the room and performed the rabble-rousing monologue from *Waiting for Lefty*. He was absolutely sensational'.

De Niro was picked to play the groom's best friend, Cecil, but was too young legally to sign the contract. He rushed home to 14th Street for his mother to look it over and OK it. Bobby was excited about his salary of $50, '...plus a percentage which, of course, I never saw anything of. I thought it was $50 *a week*, but my mother read the contract and said, "No ... it's $50." I was too young to sign it, she had to sign.'

De Niro didn't fool himself into thinking this might be a big fat break but, instead, looked at it as basically another job. 'I was doing plays from time to time, Brian was doing this low-budget film – at that time independent films seemed like something new. Well, I did it, then there were years of not doing anything.'

The film was shot hurriedly and then sat on De Palma's shelf for two more years before it was finally edited. Three years after that, after the De Niro/De Palma success of *Greetings*, it was sparingly released on the art-house circuit.

The Wedding Party is a film whose title tells a lot. Set on a Long Island estate, it's about a frantic bridegroom-to-be and his two best friends trying to handle The Ceremony. Shot in black-and-white for budget reasons its jumpy action shows the hand of a novice director and, while trying to prove himself, De Palma was actually criticised for over-directing the comedy antics of the wedding party as they wend their various ways to the church. If De Palma, De Niro and Clayburgh had not later risen to stardom, it's unlikely that this picture would ever have been shown. As De Niro would find out again in his career a few years later, once it's on film, it's history. In 1983 *The Wedding Party* was released on video-cassette to less than excited audiences who picked it up because of the new packaging which hinted it was a major De Niro/Clayburgh release. It isn't and remains a curiosity more than a success.

At the time, though, De Palma was satisfied. He'd finished a feature film with talented new actors and left the project with wider options to pursue his career. And when the opportunity came up, he brought Bobby along with him.

For the time being, though, it was business – read 'survival' –

as usual for Bobby. He went back to minor stage work and also did a walk-on in Marcel Carné's *Trois Chambres à Manhattan* but it was literally one day's work and he can barely be glimpsed in the finished product.

Bobby also deemed it a time for personal exploration and, after scraping together basic travel money, went to Europe to bum around. His father had once taken him to Paris as a young child, and he remembered the experience with delight. Anxious to expand on it with people his own age, he joined thousands of other young Americans then touring the Continent on the cheap. 'I hitched all over Europe for four months,' he later recalled in an interview, travelling from Ireland to Italy and ending up back in the City of Light. 'Yeah ... I lived in hotels near the Odéon on the Left Bank. But those French hotels are funny. They keep bumping you [cancelling reservations without warning]. Anyway, I finally found a hotel in Montmartre. I went to Alliance Français, met a lot of expatriates. The French are hard to meet. They're very private. I was in my twenties. It's a good experience to have when you're young.'

It was also an educational way to travel and work at the same time, as every experience Bobby had was stored up in his brain for possible use in some distant part. Happily, when he got back home, a new part was not all that distant when the phone rang and Brian De Palma was on the other end talking about his prospective film *Greetings*.

By 1968 De Palma had become established enough to be a part of Universal Studios' new talent programme and spent long hours trying to hatch movie plots with the programme's director, Charles Hirsch. 'Out of that frustration, smoking cigarettes and waiting for someone to return our calls, we came up with the idea for *Greetings*.'

The phrase 'Greetings from the President of the United States' has long been the opening line used on draft notices – a particularly unpopular prospect for many young and vocal Americans of the time who opposed the Vietnam War. De Palma saw a movie in this and set about plotting the story of three friends who try to avoid military induction.

The first of the three, Paul (Jonathon Warden), thinks he'll try for disqualification by pretending he's gay, while the second friend, Jon (De Niro), decides he'll masquerade as a member of a top-secret military group. The third pal, Lloyd (Gerrit Graham), is busy tracking down 'the truth' behind John Kennedy's assassination and won't be deterred from it by the draft board. Misfits all, Lloyd is dropped by the recruiters after his examination, leaving his two friends to sweat out two weeks of waiting for their evaluations.

Paul is a sex fiend who spends his time chasing computer-arranged dates, while Jon is a flagrant voyeur who spends most of his time coercing women into undressing for his camera. Jon ends up being the only one who's drafted and when he arrives in Vietnam continues his proclivities by filming Viet Cong sympathizers as they strip off their clothes.

The plot seems outlandish in retrospect but is quite of its time in reality as, during those last crazy days of the sixties, many young men resorted to anything, including leaving the country, to avoid a swampy death in South-east Asia. Bobby, as Jon, indulged himself in the eccentricities of the era and pulled his acting off with a unique craziness.

On the whole, *Greetings* turned out to be a mild success. That was due largely to De Palma's understanding of his actors. Since the three leads were basically stage-trained, he knew that there was an inherent need for improvisation, so he gave them every opportunity to do it during the miniscule shooting time of two weeks and working on a budget less than $50,000. Realizing these limits, De Palma gathered his actors for two weeks of rehearsal before a camera turned, letting them improvise dialogue into a tape-recorder.

Those sessions were the bones on which Bobby built his off-beat character, and he greatly appreciated De Palma's understanding the need of them. Unlike *The Wedding Party*, this film gave him the chance to create a character on screen that was a precursor of those to come. With his long hair, moustache and glasses, he was able to wring believable juices from his part. De Palma has said that, 'I have to have actors who can really think on their feet', and Bobby proved that this was a speciality of his.

De Palma also used his imagination in stretching his tight budget. For one important sequence he moved cast and crew to the steps of New York's Whitehall induction centre, gaining clearance by saying he was actually making a documentary on GIs. Then, after filming part of the film in 16 mm, he decided he needed 35 mm for better quality and then re-shot scenes – all within the two-week period. It was an enthusiastic madhouse but, once the film was wrapped, edited and on view – also in record time – it opened to an enthusiastic response and is now considered one of the most celebrated successes among underground/independent films of the '68-9 period; it went into the black on the New York box-office alone.

The bond between De Niro and De Palma was cemented after *Greetings*, and Bobby had honest reason to believe that a film career was possible. Though he was buried underneath the physicality of his part, the moustache, clothes etc, he was nonetheless pleased, and when he went up for a part in *Sam's Song*, he did it with ingenuous enthusiasm. After all, he tried for and got the title role – but unfortunately no one told him that was the best part of the deal.

His character, Sam, is an aspiring film-maker who shoots some things he isn't supposed to and then is set up to be killed. Too bad for Bobby that the murder happens early in the film. The real story is how his brother (Anthony Charnota) sets out to find out who did it and why. Though based on a mildly intriguing premise, the film was cheaply produced and was ignored by critics and moviegoers alike. Much later, in 1983, the project came back to haunt him when the film was found languishing in a New York City warehouse – along with unused footage of Bobby not seen in the original. This footage was grafted onto the original print and given a new title, *The Swap*, and a new advertising campaign. Then it was packaged on video-cassette and shipped out to stores with the tagline 'He's tough. He's cool. He's murder on women ... And they're death on him!' Neither the title nor the artwork, though, could disguise the fact that the film was a stinker, another video curiosity of Bobby's learning years, an embarrassment after he'd become a major star.

During all this time he'd maintained his friendship with Shelley Winters, and she often had glimpses of the real Bobby De Niro. 'He almost never shows emotion in public. But once ... years ago in New York, I gave a Thanksgiving party. Invited all my theatrical waifs, my babies. [Bobby often refers to her as 'my Jewish mother.'] Bobby was there, waiting for his date, a young actress he had a crush on. She didn't show up until dessert. She sort of floated in "Oh, hi, Bobby ...". He went into the bedroom and pounded the headboard with his fist. He was crying. He never talked to her again.'

At the time Shelley Winters was once again hot box-office, due largely to her portrayal of crazy loudmouths. In 1965 she'd received an Oscar for one of those loony ladies in *A Patch of Blue* and had followed it up with the superb *Alfie* (1966), Paul Newman's tiredly sexy *Harper* (also 1966) and, in 1967, the screen version of Neil Simon's *Enter Laughing*, followed by a rollicking harlot role opposite Burt Lancaster in *The Scalphunters*. She played parts for over-the-hill stars – and did them winningly.

Never a great beauty and seldom subdued on screen (or in public for that matter), Shelley Winters had seen her career rise and wither. It blossomed early, in 1949's *A Double Life*, followed shortly by the classic *A Place in the Sun* in which she played Montgomery Clift's ill-fated girlfriend. The early to mid 1950s saw her brief stint as a sex symbol in 1955's *The Big Knife*, and now, some fifteen years later, she basically just wanted to keep on working. To that end she was reading the script for *Bloody Mama*, a Depression era tale of the infamous Ma Barker and her hoodlum brood of sons.

American-International Pictures saw the film as a low-rent *Bonnie and Clyde*-type story beefed up by Shelley Winters' name, a combination that would hopefully grab the drive-in, double-bill crowds and wring a lot of quick money from their pockets. They wanted her badly enough to let her help cast the picture, and for the part of one of her four psychopathic sons, Lloyd Barker, she told them she wanted De Niro. The character was a real charmer, addicted to morphine and sadism and who ultimately dies of an overdose. De Niro was immediately interested, not only for Lloyd's erratic character but also because it would mark his first picture backed by a major studio. Another plus came when he learned that among his co-workers would be such respected actors as Pat Hingle, Bruce Dern, Diane Varsi and Don Stroud.

Shelley Winters recalled to Patricia Bosworth Bobby's intense need for preparation for the role, telling how he set out for the Arkansas location in an old Volkswagen so he could learn and perfect the local speech patterns necessary for Lloyd's believability. 'Bobby left for the Ozarks early so he could tape accents. Get into the character.' He stockpiled so much native knowledge that canny producer/director Roger Corman eventually used him for two jobs – as actor and as dialogue coach! Bobby and Shelley shortly got into arguments because, 'I thought he was concentrating too much on externals – I mean the things he did to his body! He is a wizard, though. He can blush or turn white just like that! But he broke out in sores. He refused to eat and drank only water – he must've lost thirty pounds. Just to *look* like an addict.

'Oh, and he almost got us killed. In one scene he had to drive us in this car. The cameras roll. Suddenly we're careering around this field, and it's like he's out of control at the wheel. I whispered, "Bobby, do you know how to drive?" and he grinned. "Are you kidding? I'm from New York. Why would I know how to drive?" I started screaming. Afterward Roger Corman wanted to shoot another take, but I took him aside and explained that if we did he might lose two important members of the cast.'

Joking aside, De Niro's obsessive need to get into character shortly made her a nervous wreck. Lloyd '...was supposed to deteriorate physically but Bobby got so frail we all became alarmed. At night we'd all go out and stuff ourselves, and Bobby would just sit, drinking water. When he gets to the soul of a character, he refuses to let it go. This is going to sound crazy,' she told Marie Brenner, 'but ... Bobby got killed in *Bloody Mama*. His part was over. He could have gone home. On the day we were to shoot the burial scene, I walked over to the open grave, looked down and got the shock of my life. "Bobby!" I screamed. "I don't believe this! You get out of that grave this minute!" ' To see the character through to the end, he had actually got down into the pit and half covered himself with dirt so that his fellow actors would look down and get an honest reaction.

The buzz from the five-week shoot emphasized how well Bobby and Shelley were getting along, so much so that gossip hinted at a romantic involvement well over and above simple friendship. She now denies that anything of the kind occurred, saying, 'Call him the son I never had, call him ... Listen, he needed to be taken care of. Yeah I guess Bobby looked up to me in those days.'

When it was released, *Bloody Mama* did indeed become a drive-in success, chock full as it was of car chases, some gratuitous sex, bloody shoot-outs and the authenticity of its locations, but it didn't do much for anyone's career. Bobby was pleased, though, later saying that, after all, it '…was the first big movie I had ever done. Low budget by Hollywood standards I guess – but it was a 35 mm production with antique cars, well-known actors …' In short, all the hours of preparation had paid off by his getting his feet wet in Hollywood waters.

One positive result of *Bloody Mama* was that Shelley had more faith in Bobby's talent than ever. She was then finishing writing a semi-autobiographical stage piece consisting of three short, separate plays which took place at various times during an actress's life. It was to be called *One Night Stands of a Noisy Passenger,* and she decided that Bobby would be perfect for the male lead in the third instalment, called *Last Stand.*

The three playlets covered three intense relationships in the life of an Oscar-winning actress from budding talent to self-destructive, ageing star. In *Last Stand*, Diane Ladd played the star as her career was nose-diving and excitement seemed the only palliative. De Niro plays her unlikely diversion, a karate-chopping, bisexual and would-be Method actor whom she meets and beds one night during an acid trip. Bizarre? Certainly. Challenging? Definitely so, as De Niro proved when he began studying karate immediately and within weeks was able to pull off the stunt of breaking a board in two – all for a sequence that lasted only fifteen seconds on stage.

Laced with four-letter words, the playlet was a gritty look at the life of Hollywood in the late 1960s, when hippies roamed the avenues and often the bedrooms of its stars. When it opened in December 1970, De Niro again received those 'keep-your-eyes-on-this-guy' type of reviews, but one of his best notices came from Shelley Winters herself, who was practically slack-mouthed in her approval of his roaring performance. 'It was like watching sexual lightning on stage. Every night was a different performance.'

On the whole, however, critics savaged the play, and the lights at the Actor's Playhouse were quickly dark, a fact that Shelley did not take well. 'What can I tell you?' she asked after reading the newspapers on the morning after. 'I've been clobbered and I'm in a daze. Nobody understands my plays' – particularly critic Richard Watts, who stated that she was 'a simply dreadful dramatist', while another opined that she '… makes sex so ugly and dull that even the most ardent voyeur would be turned off by this trio of tawdry peepshows'.*

Luckily for De Niro, he didn't have just a set of reviews from a failed play to keep him company, as earlier in the year he'd made another film with Brian De Palma which was then surfacing.

During production it was playfully called *Son of Greetings*, since it was virtually a sequel to their earlier effort. *Greetings* had been successful enough for De Palma to get a better deal on this picture – twice the money and double the shooting-time. He wanted De Niro to play the further adventures of Jon Rubin, the voyeur now home from the war and seeking new excitement. Bobby was delighted at the idea and immediately accepted, even though the money was small. What excited him was being able to expand a character he'd already created and take it into new areas.

The plot of *Hi, Mom!*, the film's ultimate title, had Rubin now a budding film-maker who sets up his camera in his New York apartment and aims it at a neighbouring building where he captures the daily routines of several of its residents, including a revolutionary student, an 'average' family, a playboy and his live-in girlfriend and, finally, a group of young women who share an apartment. Rubin's character now has a chance to integrate his innate voyeurism into his 'work' and he gleefully looks forward to making a public statement out of his private fascinations.

In one funny scene, he manages to seduce one of the women into his apartment and into his bed, all the while covertly filming the action. It's only after she's gone that he finds out his camera has slipped and missed the big scene completely. After that fiasco, he turned his attention to the stage. Teaming with the revolutionary student he's been spying on, who is white but espouses the Black movement, he films a performance of a radical production called *Be Black Baby* – during which its all-white audience is heckled and assaulted. Eventually the actors storm the building Rubin's been photographing and it's destroyed. When television newsmen catch him in front of the wrecked structure, Rubin blithely suggests that it could only have been the work of a seasoned demolition expert, an art he had specialized in during the war.

---

* After reviews like that it's a wonder that Shelley was able to regroup her powers to write her hugely successful autobiography, *Shelley Also Known as Shirley*, in 1983. She did and is also planning a follow-up book.

It was an uneven picture, in and out of production for months, but it's saved by De Niro's bristling vitality and manic personality. He got to ham it up, mugging and improvising all over the screen to his heart's content. That's what De Palma wanted and that's exactly what he got.

Years later, in London, an interviewer asked him if he'd seen the film recently but, by then a world-class superstar, he didn't especially want to be reminded of his 'experimental' film period. Just the idea of it was '...a little scary. I didn't want to look at it because it would remind me of things – like the first time you ever hear your own voice or the first time I ever saw myself on film ... I don't need to see it.'

Undoubtedly he feels the same about two more screen appearances that came his way then. *Jennifer On My Mind* was a grim drama about drug-addiction which saw him doing brief duty as a taxi-driver (shades of things to come?), and *Born To Win*. *Born* ... was another drug picture, albeit a black-comedy look at the subject, and starred George Segal and Karen Black. De Niro played a rough-'em-up cop in this, but if you went out for popcorn, you missed his scenes. Its original title was *Scraping Bottom*, which is what several critics thought was exactly what it did.

Bobby knew these films weren't going to do much for him but there was always the challenge inherent in working that intrigued him. He was *working*, and that was truly the most important thing. Where others might have been discouraged by the fact that the 'big break' kept eluding him, Bobby never lost faith. 'I never became disillusioned,' he said later. 'I knew that if I kept at it I would at least make a decent living. If you are half-way decent at what you do, by the law of averages, in five or ten years, you will make enough money to do what you want to.' Though stardom still seemed a distant goal, De Niro was obviously already assessing its possible rewards, not for their own sake but for the power of choice that success would bring. He was definitely coming to terms with the facts of life of acting for a living, and he was positive he could master them.

3 Back and Forth from Little Italy

As the 1970s got fully underway, De Niro was a happy man. He was professional enough to read the writing on the wall (his many good reviews) and to appreciate the close friends he'd made, such as Shelley Winters and Brian De Palma. Also the cramped apartment on Fourteenth Street now boasted several movie posters with his name on them, and while he never displayed them to friends, they were reminders of the steps he'd taken and a source of enthusiasm for what would be ahead in the new decade.

When he was offered a part in *The Gang That Couldn't Shoot Straight*, he took it with relish, particularly because it was about Little Italy and gangsters, two arenas of society he had been able to observe all his life. The part called for an authentic Calabrian accent, and that was all De Niro needed to hear before packing a bag and taking off for Italy with his trusty tape-recorder to get down the real thing. Again one could appreciate his dedication, but for a picture like this it seemed too generous.

The story is a zany telling of the misadventures of Salvatore 'Kid Sally' Palumbo and his bumbling gang of misfits as they attempt to improve their image amidst the underworld rivalry of Brooklyn's various Mafia 'families'. One way they are trying to do this is by sponsoring a bicycle race amongst themselves, but to make sure their team has the advantage, they import a cyclist from Italy – that was to be De Niro. 'Kid Sally', played with relish by Broadway actor Jerry Ohrbach, doesn't realize, however, that this particular import is also a determined kleptomaniac, not to mention also being a would-be seducer instantly interested in the 'Kid's' sister, played by a dewy-faced Leigh Taylor-Young. The gang also gets involved with a lion that's used to terrorize local businesses the gang 'protects' and, ultimately, the police. Everyone ends up in prison except De

Niro's Mario, who impersonates a priest and then makes his way back home.

While many people, including the story's original author, Jimmy Breslin, considered the film to be a waste of time and talent, it was sporadically quite funny, due mostly to De Niro's goofy performance. He later admitted that he was taking all offers coming his way at the time but that this film was a low point. 'With *The Gang That Couldn't Shoot Straight* I liked the part, but the movie was done badly.' He did get the best of the reviews, though, and practically stole the picture from Ohrbach and the rest of the cast, including Lionel Stander and Jo Van Fleet.

By now, De Niro's basic acting style was beginning to set, although he still insisted on going through the manoeuvres he'd learned in class and was most comfortable with. This was particularly evident when he began rehearsals for another Off-Broadway play, *Schubert's Last Serenade*, directed by Julie Bovasso, a seasoned actress who later rose to movie prominence playing John Travolta's mother in *Saturday Night Fever*. He was cast as a construction worker in this comic farce, who falls for an uppity college girl, and dug his heels into finding his character from the word go. 'For the first week or so of rehearsal I thought, "Oh my poor play",' Julie Bovasso remembered. She was initially aghast at De Niro's approach to the part, saying, 'He arrives at his characterization by what seems like a very circuitous route.' The play takes place primarily in a restaurant and, 'he wanted to do one scene while chewing on breadsticks. Dubiously I let him and for three days I didn't hear a word of my play – it was all garbled up in breadsticks.'

Patience being the main virtue of a director, Julie Bovasso let him mumble and explore, swallowing her own nervousness as she could sense that something positive was emerging. 'He was making a connection with something, a kind of clown element. At dress rehearsal he showed up without the breadsticks. I said, "Bobby, where are they?" And he said simply, "I don't need them anymore." '

It seemed that the acting principles he'd been soaking up since he was a teenager were paying off and that whatever scars may have remained from his lonely childhood had been turned into physical badges of insight and understanding.

His choppy good looks, his lean frame, mumbly voice and

piercing eyes were now all tools of his trade as a journeyman actor whose reputation was growing more solid with each new play or movie. Yet, underneath any façade he might take on, De Niro remained himself. Charles Maryan, who directed him in the plays *Billy Bailey* and *The Great American Refrigerator*, put it this way: 'He is simply not show business. People who don't know him think he's somewhere else, but he is very much *there* – soaking up new characters, new situations. He is always watching, observing.' Maryan's remarks came later in De Niro's career but they were as true then as now. His personal life was secondary to his work, and while he liked it that way, there's also the fact that he was an actor and half-Jewish, which undoubtedly didn't endear him to the mothers of Little Italy with marriageable daughters. The women in his acting life were closest, but instead of turning into flaming romances, his relationships with the likes of Shelley Winters and Sally Kirkland soon coalesced into fast and enduring friendships. If De Niro was suffering from sleepless nights, it was because his thoughts were always centred on the *next* part, the *next* break.

Before many more quiet nights had passed, though, he did indeed have a new acting opportunity, and it would be a part that loosened him up emotionally on screen for the first time. His character? Bruce Pearson. The project? *Bang the Drum Slowly*.

Bang the Drum Slowly began its media life as a novel in 1956, followed shortly by a one-hour television dramatization starring Paul Newman. Now, in 1973, it was set to make the transition to the big screen, and De Niro was deemed just the right man to bring the doomed baseball catcher, Bruce Pearson, to this new dimension.

The story is basically about Pearson's acceptance of Hodgkins Disease and his attempts to enjoy the remainder of his days and to get his life in order. To help him he needs a friend, and team-mate Henry Wiggen, played warmly by Michael Moriarty, is the one he turns to. In fact, most of the film's action is seen through Wiggen's eyes as he tries to help his friend both adjust to and accept his circumstances, thus providing De Niro's character with an empty canvas on which to come alive, warts and all.

It was virtually the first time on screen that De Niro's character was a sympathetic one, and the film's tender moments are all the more powerful for that. One particularly haunting

scene comes after his diagnosis, when he takes his friend
Wiggen back home and then one night, in the back yard of his
parents' house, slowly feeds a small fire with the newspaper
accounts of his career and acknowledges its imminent end. Also
Wiggen defends him to both the team and its owners, insisting
that whatever happens to Bruce happens to him also. Since
Bruce is not that great a catcher and Wiggen is one of the team
stars, people shortly begin to wonder why he's being so
generous. Simple friendship is the answer – and Bruce is sorely
in need of a friend, as he says, shakily, to Wiggen, 'I've never
been smart. That's the thing.'

Wiggen attempts to open up the dying man's life by making
his team-mates more companionable and also by taking care of
his large life-insurance policy. Bruce, bedazzled by the slightly
faded charms of a Southern belle (played with dangerous charm
by the remarkable Ann Wedgeworth), wants to leave everything
to her but Wiggen vetoes that move and she drops out of
Bruce's life. When his fellow ballplayers come to know that he's
dying, they too rally around, making him truly one of the gang.
De Niro's Pearson responds to this sudden upswing in
acceptance with a wondering, tobacco-chewing smile, hardly
able to grasp that he's finally a welcome part of the group. As he
gets closer to the end, his sincerity becomes almost palpable.
The predictable finale is still able to bring a lump to the throat,
and Robert De Niro emerged as a true film force to be reckoned
with.

Not that he hadn't worked to make it play that way, to make it
look *that* easy. By now serious homework was a basic part of his
acting life, and he told *American Film* magazine exactly how he
was able to convince audiences that he was the dying ballplayer
who captured moviegoers' hearts.

'I went down South with a tape-recorder and got local people
to go over the whole script with me. Then I was always
watching for little traits that I could use. And then I did all the
baseball. We practiced in [New York's] Central Park for, I think,
three weeks to a month. When I was in Florida, I practiced a lot,
even with the batting machines. I also watched ball games on
television. You're looking right at the catcher all the time, and
you can see how relaxed he is, in a sense.'

The most personally disgusting research De Niro had to do
was to perfect the art of chewing tobacco. 'It was a bad

experience,' he later recalled. 'Somebody told me to mix the tobacco with bubble gum. Then I got sticky *and* sick. Finally a local doctor told me that chewing tobacco would make my teeth white. That gave me the courage to keep chewing. I got so I could *look* like I enjoyed it. But it didn't do a thing for my teeth.'

The evolution of the film was peculiarly 'Hollywood' in its conception. Paramount had owned the rights to the book for some time but it wasn't until director John Hancock came along that they were finally ready to proceed. Hancock had just come off a successful horror number, *Let's Scare Jessica to Death*, and agreed to do *Bang the Drum...* only if he could cast newcomers so the story would seem all the more authentic. After many auditions, he picked an outstanding group of actors, including Selma Diamond, Phil Foster (later to achieve fame as Laverne's dad on television's *Laverne and Shirley*). Barbara Babcock and, as the team's coach, Vincent Gardenia.

Casting the lead roles took longer, however, with De Niro later admitting, 'I read for the director about seven times. I read first for Michael Moriarty's part, then I read for the part I played I read for the director, the producer, the producer and his wife and finally I got the part. I kind of felt I deserved it after that.'

The finished product, which took some eighteen months off and on to complete, was greeted as one of the finest movies of the year, and De Niro's sensitive portrayal of the slow-witted catcher was a critical hit. One said that his Pearson '...is wonderfully exasperating, one of the most unsympathetic characters ever to win an audience's sympathy'. He won the 1973 New York Film Critics Award, and it seemed a distinct possibility that an Oscar might follow. It didn't happen, though Vincent Gardenia's performance as the gruff but understanding coach of the mythical Mammoths ball club did win him a Best Supporting nomination and brought more publicity to the film.

About *Bang the Drum...*, De Niro feels: 'I thought I did OK. It's always hard to be objective.' All he was sure of at the time was that he'd shared top billing in a successful major studio film and for his efforts received a major acting award. His level of recognizability was growing daily, and the respect he was gaining from his co-workers was also on the rise. Director Hancock was amazed at the actor's sense of dedication and almost reverence for the part – 'He didn't even want to take the uniform off' – and later told *Observer* magazine that, 'He reminds

me of Alec Guinness, submerging himself totally in his role ...
Guinness isn't a personality actor, he's a character actor who is
also a star – and that's Bobby. But he has an eroticism Guinness
never had.'

And once people met De Niro and built a friendship or even
just worked with him they didn't forget him. A monumental
example of this had come over Christmas 1971, when writer Jay
Cocks and his actress wife, Verna Bloom, threw a holiday party.
They had no idea that in doing so they'd be bringing together
two talents that would make movie history, for among the
group of partygoers were De Niro and another pal of the Cocks,
a young director named Martin Scorsese.

The son of Italian immigrants and who himself had been
raised in Little Italy, Scorsese was the kind of man who always
had his nose to the ground and his eyes peeled for interesting
characters. As a director, that was part of his business, and he
was very good at it. As a child he too had spent many an
afternoon immersed in the movies with his father, soaking up a
wide range of films, from glossy musicals to Technicolored
dramas. 'I even saw *Duel in the Sun*, which was condemned by
the [Catholic] Church when it came out.' He was born in 1942 in
Flushing, New York, but his parents moved back to their local
roots of Little Italy when he was ten, and he became wildly
attracted to movies when his asthma condition prevented his
taking part in sports or other physical activities.

Intensely cerebral, Scorsese lived out his budding emotions
on the screens of his youth in the cinematic company of the stars
of the time. He had wanted to be a priest but his poor health
ruled that out, as it did the other common occupation of young
Italians – the business of becoming a gangster. Therefore movies
turned into his primary way of escaping from reality, and
eventually he began to think what he could do with a group of
stars if *he* was the one making them move around and across the
screen.

When Cocks introduced his two guests, De Niro and
Scorsese, to each other, Martin was initially dumbstruck. He
could hardly believe it but he recognized Bobby from the streets
of his childhood – the very ones Bobby had warily trod.

'Hey!' he said. 'Didn't you use to hang out around Hester
Street?' De Niro stared silently back – '...just stared at me – he
doesn't look at you, he *considers* you – so I stared back. Then I

remembered: "It was Kenmare Street – the Kenmare gang." And Bobby goes, "Heh heh!" I hadn't seen him in fourteen years.'

This sharing of experiences, plus their Italian outlook on life and their unabashed love of movies, quickly made the pair close friends. There was an instinctive trust between them, since, 'We were both guys who'd grown up on the street.' The only real difference between them was Scorsese's volubility and De Niro's introspectiveness. 'Bobby hardly talked at all. I might be rambling on, and suddenly I'd notice that Bobby had fallen fast asleep!'

By that point in his career, Scorsese had directed only five minor films but his desire to enlarge his talent was equal to De Niro's and slowly he found '...that we could improvise on anything ... Bobby was quite a clown.'* That shared sense of humour was the spine that would support their long-running working relationship, involving, as it would, many unsavoury topics.

Humour is just the opposite of violence, and the many shades of violence (as reflected in the faces of *Mean Streets'* manic Johnny Boy, *Taxi Driver's* homicidal saviour Travis Bickle, *Raging Bull's* Jake La Motta, and the pathetic star-stalker Rupert Pupkin of *The King of Comedy*) were to be the coin of their cinematic realm, relieved only briefly by the tarnished emotions of *New York, New York*.

De Niro had seen and appreciated Scorsese's film *Who's That Knocking at My Door?* – '...I thought it was terrific. Then I heard he was doing *Mean Streets*. We talked about a few of the parts and I couldn't make up my mind which I wanted to play. I ran into Harvey Keitel in the street – he was going to play Charlie – he said, "You'd be terrific as Johnny Boy." At first I thought I should ask for the lead part, but it doesn't work that way. It might not be right career-wise, but I felt it was important to work with people I respected and Marty was one of them.' And that's been a basic rule of De Niro's ever since.

Mean Streets was the first of the five films the pair have made so far, and De Niro's insight into their working relationship was right on target. Not only did he admire Scorsese's work but he

* Years later, when television promotion of films became a necessity, 'We'd improvise the questions Gene Shalit might ask us on the *Today Show* and we'd die laughing.'

admired the man as well, and their sharing of similar family histories almost made him the brother De Niro never had.

When they began talking about *Mean Streets* and it was decided that Johnny Boy would be the part De Niro would play, he promptly dived into his prop room and came up with precisely the kind of porkpie hat that his wiseguy character would likely wear. Obviously there was more to it than that, but Scorsese was later to joke that, 'He was wearing a hat and tilted it a certain way, saying he thought the character would wear it that way.' In any case it's an early example of his being prepared. His secondhand-shop days were paying off. 'Costumes can look too created,' Scorsese reflected. 'When I saw that crazy hat, I knew he'd be perfect.'

Mean Streets wasn't an easy project to put together. Shortly after the pair met at that party, Scorsese went on to his first mainline moneymaker, 1972's *Boxcar Bertha*, yet another Depression-era Grade B *Bonnie and Clyde*. Starring the exquisite Barbara Hershey, it was a popular hit on the drive-in and double-bill circuit and established Scorsese as a director with an eye towards what the public wanted to see. This accolade came from no less an expert than the film's producer, Roger Corman, himself an experienced master of sensing audience trends and capitalizing on them, from his horror-picture cycle of the early sixties to the then-current gangster craze whose success originated in part with his film with De Niro, *Bloody Mama*.

Corman was so pleased with *Bertha*'s gross profits that he offered Scorsese another directing job, on another exploitation number called *I Escaped From Devil's Island* – an overly sadistic response to the then-popular *Papillon*. Scorsese had other ideas. After completing work on *Boxcar Bertha*, he'd had the opportunity to work with one of Hollywood's true characters, John Cassavetes, on his *Minnie and Moskovitz*, and came away with the advice to avoid exploitation pictures and make more personal ones. For Cassavetes that route had led to intermittent success but great personal reward – something he wanted Scorsese to experience in his own way.

With that in his mind, Scorsese went to his files and picked up the first draft of *Mean Streets*, which he'd co-written with Martin Mardik back in 1966. To him the story was almost a flipside companion-piece to *The Godfather*, which had just recently become a smash hit. But while that film was centred on the highest echelons of the gangster lifestyle, *Mean Streets* was to be as tense and exciting as its title suggested.

For financing the project he went to his friend Jonathon Taplin, who managed Bob Dylan and The Band. Together they made a deal and, according to Scorsese, 'What eventually happened was that Taplin liked the script and we got to make the film with the same Corman crew from *Boxcar Bertha*.*

The budget was tiny (under a half million dollars), matched only by a shooting schedule of twenty-seven days – with an extra ten for rehearsal. Of those twenty-seven, only six were actually spent shooting on location in New York. The remainder were used up on a Hollywood soundstage where the major set, Tony's Bar, was constructed. It was particularly ironic that the *business* of making movies forced them to do most of it some 3,000 miles away from the twisted, crowded and emotional territory of their youth – especially since that neighbourhood was what the film was all about.

Conversely their sparse shooting-time and limited budget did help speed up the lightning-paced story of a hyperactive street hood named Johnny Boy and the friend who tries to bring him into line and back into the 'family'.

Before filming began, De Niro haunted the streets of his youth, looking for clues to his character, Johnny Boy. 'I met a lot of people and knew someone in particular who the character was based on. I talked to people who knew him, so I got a composite. Then I followed my instincts.' And they paid off as he breathed life into a character described in the script as a 'punk bastard' seemingly bent on self-destruction.

De Niro's Johnny Boy is an exotic mixture of rough, untrammelled sex-appeal and low-mentality street cunning who slides through life under-estimating the ferocity of his own kind, including his friends. He's a loser who doesn't know he's behind in the game, or as Charlie, played by Harvey Keitel, puts it, 'Who knows what goes on in that kid's head?' as he tried to explain away Johnny Boy's erratic behaviour. The base of Johnny Boy's troubles is that he's deeply in debt to a number of

---

* Scorsese was quick to acknowledge his Roger Corman education and gave him a tribute in *Mean Streets*. Whenever Johnny Boy and his friend Charlie went to the movies, it was to the 42nd Street 'grind houses' (cheap 24-hour theatres) in Manhattan, and on screen was always playing a Corman double bill, usually starring Vincent Price.

his cronies, and while that might have been worked out, he continues to borrow and spend, showing no respect for his peers – and that's the point from which he finds there's no return.

The film is redolent with scenes from Bobby's own youth, particularly the main setting of an average downtown Italian bar. The habitués of 'Tony's' range from homosexual gangster-groupies (to be ignored and then ridiculed in the obligatory Italian-macho homophobic fashion) to visiting women from uptown who are there to ogle and tease the natives. This seamy action was backed up and energized by a string of sixties rock 'n' roll favourites – 'Hey, Mr Postman', 'If It's in His Kiss' etc – which perfectly set both the time of the story and the rambunctious personalities who found those anthems to their raucous lives.

In the climactic car chase, Johnny Boy is shot in the jugular vein by a mysterious killer hired by his old gang – a part played by Scorsese. Like Alfred Hitchcock and others before him, he also has a penchant for popping up in his own films – and sometime later he'd play another mysterious stranger in the back of Travis Bickle's taxi.

From its first screening to its theatrical release, the buzz on *Mean Streets* was noisy and positive. Critics were astonished by De Niro's explosion onto the screen and his manic exposure of uncontrolled energy as Johnny Boy. Also applauded was Scorsese's direction, with writers saying that he '...perfectly evokes the sordid realities of New York's Little Italy' and adding that it was '...as if he simply went out there alone in his own world with a camera'.

There was an essence of truth in that last statement considering the roots of the director, De Niro and Harvey Keitel, and their ability, during the ten days of rehearsal, to improvise much of the action. When De Niro was later asked about this making-it-up-on-the-spot, he replied that it was partly true but that, after any successful improvising, 'We would then rehearse and then set it very clearly. Otherwise it would have been all over the place ... sometimes we'd do things that were a little scary, but – it's only the movies.'

He also found his initial trust in Scorsese as a director to be well justified. 'He's not afraid to make choices that possibly other directors would not want to make. We just understand each other without having to go into a lot of discussion, but when we do discuss, we come up with something.' Obviously the feeling was mutual, as *Mean Streets* proved to be just the first collaboration between the pair; over the next years they would make four more films together.

Before their reunion, however, there was another part in particular just waiting for Robert De Niro, one that would carefully keep his rambunctious mongrel energy on a tight lead. Francis Ford Coppola was putting together a sequel to his monster hit *The Godfather*, and the script was structured to include a prequel sequence that would require the services of an actor capable of believably playing godfather Vito Corleone as a young man. To precede Marlon Brando's Oscar-winning characterization, the role was vital to the new film and would be pivotal in the career of the actor who played it. De Niro was ready to try, though admittedly awed at the possibility of emulating his acting idol. It would be the greatest challenge of his young career, and his subsequent mastery of it would make him a full-fledged star.

4   De Niro, Brando and The Godfather

Marlon Brando won the Best Actor Academy Award of 1972 for his portrayal of Mafia kingpin Vito Corleone in *The Godfather*. For him it was the part long needed to shore up a wasting career and reputation which had been sidelined for years because of his lack of interest in scripts submitted to him, an ever-expanding waistline and an increasing sense of reclusiveness that had led him to sequester himself and his sprawling family on a remote island in the South Pacific. *The Godfather* was a badly needed comeback for him, as prior to it he'd become something of a Hollywood joke, not to mention being a far cry from the acting icon of Bobby De Niro's youth.

The saying 'You're only as good as your last picture' was fast becoming Brando's professional epitaph after a long string of embarrassing flops, ranging from 1968's *Candy* to *The Night of the Following Day* (1969), 1970's *Burn* and 1971's concocted prequel to *The Turn of the Screw*, entitled *The Nightcomers*. He had made huge salaries from these, however, and even if his movies were poor and virtually ignored by the public, he was rich enough not to have to care. Instead, he just sat back among his South Sea concubines and collection of children and turned off the outside world, declaring that he could live happily without acting as he considered it to be an unimportant and neurotic profession. In short, the sexually magnetic Stanley Kowalski of *A Streetcar Named Desire* was just a dim memory. Brando's leeringly sensuous face and sculpted body were strictly a television *Late Show* reality. In person he was barely recognizable as the same man, let alone the much-lauded actor.

What he did still have was a superstar name, but the moneymen behind *The Godfather* didn't think that was enough to cast him in their picture. By that point he had burned most of his Hollywood bridges and, in turn, Hollywood thought of him as an unpredictable and often unprofessional has-been – that is, when it thought of him at all.

Francis Coppola made them change their mind. Brando was hot to make the picture and agreed to make what was virtually a screen test to get it. Stuffing his cheeks with cotton but otherwise without make-up, he stepped in front of Francis' camera and transformed himself into the craggy, mumbly, sharklike Vito Corleone.

The two of them went on to make movie history, with Brando reinstituting himself as a major talent, if briefly, by winning the Oscar. That award, besides being deserved, was also a symbol of Hollywood's willingness to welcome him back into the mainstream, but he wasn't anxious to return to the fold. Instead he went to Paris to star in Bernardo Bertolucci's controversial *Last Tango in Paris* and then quietly returned to the South Seas.

And now here was little Bobby De Niro being asked to play a young Brando in a sequel to one of the most important films of the decade. What an incredible place to be! And who could have conceived of its happening? Certainly not the youngster who had spent hours of his youth studying Brando on the screen, first as a star to watch in awe and now as a fellow actor whose performance he'd dissect and emulate. If ever an actor had a challenge, this was it, for De Niro felt that he had not only to do justice to Brando's characterization but to make his own version as personal as possible.

Meanwhile critics were feasting off the diverse images of 'the Mob' as presented by *The Godfather* and *Mean Streets*. Many felt that Coppola's vision of New York's crime families benefited from its patina of time and distance, set as it was in the post-World War II years. This sense of the past made its violence palatable to the public, whereas the raw outrages of *Mean Streets* were of the moment. While it was highly praised for its 'honesty', people did not line up to see it. Certainly it was not the fault of the director or stars, for they had done their job extremely well, perhaps too much so.

New York in the early seventies was a precarious place. Apartments were still stabilized under Second World War rent-control laws, and for those with enough money to buy a brownstone house, gentrification of old neighbourhoods was well underway. People were looking ahead and in many cases ignoring the present in anticipation of this hopeful future. If there were still gangs in Little Italy, so what? New Yorkers didn't want to know from it, especially those who'd just invested life-savings in houses and repairs. When they went to neighbourhoods like Little Italy, they were looking for a good meal and not a gang shoot-out. As seen through *The Godfather*, they could accept its reality through a gauzy mist of things past. *Mean Streets*, on the other hand, left the spectre of urban violence right on their doorsteps, and most people simply stepped over it and tried to forget it was there.

Coppola's success with *The Godfather* was phenomenal, and it proved to be the movie event of the year. Singlehandedly he had brought back a movie genre that many in the money chairs of Hollywood had thought not only dead but buried as well. There may have been the exception on the drive-in circuit (as per *Bloody Mama*) but serious moviegoers were deemed unaffected until this film broke that notion in tiny pieces. The most positive proof came in the box-office, which eventually raked in over $84.5 million in North America alone. *Mean Streets* didn't gross the $4 million necessary to get on the movie hit list.

Hollywood, and Paramount in particular, thought Coppola was on the crest of a wave, yet his next film, *The Conversation*, was a well-reviewed flop, and his script for *The Great Gatsby* contributed to a film that the buzz in Hollywood nicknamed 'The Great Ghastly'. It was only a matter of time before a sequel to *The Godfather* was brought up.

Coppola was interested in doing a sequel – but only under certain conditions. Since his original hit, he had been deluged by personal feelings that his film had romanticized what one critic called his 'indulgent story of the highest levels of the politics of crime'. This was never his intention, and to dispel it he decided that the second *Godfather* movie would be constructed in such a way as to deglamourize the Corleone family and show it as the bloody *business* it really was. 'The Mafia,' said Coppola, 'is no different from any other big greedy, profit-making corporation in America.'

In this sequel he was especially interested in conveying the sense of tradition that marks underworld families and decided to start this film off with the genesis of the mighty Corleones – the young Vito and how he evolved into becoming the godfather of his immediate world.

To do this he needed an actor who could convey the honest evolution of Vito Corleone and also one who could believably be a 'young' Marlon Brando. This was no part for any popular fan magazine-made star. It *was* a part for a strong and independent young actor who would be able to understand the complexities required and bring his own strength to it. It was a part for Robert De Niro.

After Coppola saw him in *Mean Streets*, his genius allowed him to recognize the flexibility of De Niro's talent, and their creation of the youthful Vito Corleone was virtually the flip side of Johnny Boy. Instead of being an overcocky, loutish street tough who blows up mailboxes for the fun of it, De Niro's Vito was quiet and deadly cool, almost slinking across the screen rather than overwhelming it as he had in *Mean Streets*.

But it did not happen without careful preparation. Once De Niro and Coppola came to terms, Bobby began extensively to research this new character, seeking clues to his own portrayal in Brando's own. He confessed to friends that it was arduous work and, while intimidated by Brando's stamp on the part, was determined to bring his own personal mark to it.

He began by studying Brando's ageing Don Corleone by the hour, re-running *The Godfather* some fifty times searching out keys to his characterization. Journeying to Sicily, he attempted to research the character's roots, and while he didn't find out any secrets of the Mafia, he did come away with a Sicilian accent that was so perfect he was mistaken for a native.

De Niro also studied Brando's old films and the newer one, but he practically memorized *The Godfather* until he could imitate Brando perfectly. Yet he wanted – and needed – more than that, as he had to turn back Brando's clock and *become* the younger version, completely assimilating body mannerisms and vocal characterizations until he'd developed a complete alphabet of Brando's persona. 'I didn't [just] want to do an imitation of Brando,' he later exclaimed, 'but I wanted to make it believable that I could be him as a young man. It was like a mathematical problem.' Once that was in place, he was able to draw on it like a private savings account, reforging speech patterns and body movements into ones recognizable as the character's yet still distinctly his own. A complicated process, it also was one that met with ultimate success.

Coppola was a sympathetic director to De Niro, even though

the actor reportedly drove him crazy with his constant questions, always on the look-out for a new avenue of approach or nuance of attitude.

His sequence in *The Godfather Part II* was relatively short, considering the film ran some three hours and twenty minutes when finished, yet the entire movie hinged on his performance, as Vito's youth was the touchstone of the Corleone empire, and believability was of the essence. The story of the young Vito's introduction into the criminal life was interspersed between the current stages of the family's saga, and it all worked beautifully in the final version.

Audiences flocked to *The Godfather Part II* primarily because of the popularity of the original – audiences really wanted to know more about the Corleones – but they all walked away dumbstruck by the screen presence of De Niro. They *believed* they were actually seeing the young Vito grow from the uncertain immigrant of New York's turn-of-the-century mean streets into the stocky, tuxedoed Don Corleone as depicted by Brando.

Critics were once again in awe as they watched the brash young De Niro languidly slip into the skin of his part, never overtly commanding but plainly presenting a quiet and rock-hard power as the fledgeling criminal who learns how the system works by being, initially, a victim of it and then inserting himself into a place of power by assassinating the old gangster Fanucci during a religious street festival. The counterbalance between the solemnity of the festival and young Vito's stalking of his prey from overlooking rooftops is both startlingly dramatic and violent.*

Sequels, no matter how well done, are seldom the financial equal to the original, and *The Godfather Part II* proved no exception. It did gross some $30.6 million, though, and was lavishly acknowledged when Oscar nominations were announced. It received the same number of nominations as the first movie – nine in all. Both films won the Best Picture Award, and the part of Vito Corleone, whatever his age, seemed upstoppable: Brando had won Best Actor in 1972 and De Niro

* De Niro's participation took on added importance when Coppola eventually took his two films, added previously unused footage and grafted together a ten-hour *Godfather* mini-series for television which told the Corleone story in sequence. Considering this series, there are actually three *Godfather* films.

Best Supporting Actor two years later in the first instance of the Academy's voting awards to two actors playing the same part. An added irony was that one of De Niro's co-nominees in his category was Lee Strasberg, nominated for his role as the ageing crime tsar in *The Godfather Part II*. It was the first time in history that an actor had been in competition with a former teacher, and winning to boot!

But that year De Niro's category was crammed with great performances. Besides Strasberg, he was up against another *Godfather* graduate, Michael V. Gazzo, Jeff Bridges in *Thunderbolt and Lightfoot*, and the sentimental favourite, Fred Astaire, for his work in *The Towering Inferno*. With the possible exception of Astaire, the nominations were well deserved but the mystique of *The Godfather Part II* – as epitomized by De Niro's acting – won the day.

By Oscar night De Niro had departed for a long location shoot in Italy for *1900*, and his award was accepted by Coppola, who crowed that he was happy 'one of my boys made it'. He later added that he was so impressed with Bobby's work that, 'I would not hestiate to cast [him] in any role whatsoever – from a little street rat to Valentino.'

There were rumours that the film's nominal star (and longtime De Niro friend), Al Pacino, had spoken to Coppola about keeping De Niro off the picture as he was afraid that his own presence would be wiped off the screen. He was wrong, as he received a Best Actor nomination, although De Niro did get a landslide of publicity.

At one point early on in establishing his character, Bobby had admitted to a friend of Brando's just how thorough the latter's work had been and that, 'There's only one thing I can do: I have to do Brando. I have to imitate Brando rather than create a new character.' When Brando's pal passed this along, he replied, 'I can understand how he would want to do that, but he won't be able to.' It took Brando's seeing the finished product to convince him that Bobby could do that and more. He left the theatre saying that De Niro was '...the most talented actor working today. I doubt if he knows how good he is.'

That was high praise, matched perhaps only by that of Lee Strasberg. His Hyman Roth in *The Godfather Part II* was a study in fatigued and jaded reality as he played the dying Jewish mobster, but would he have liked to have won the Oscar?

Probably. Was he sorry he didn't? No. 'Bobby deserves it, and he'll get it.'

As to De Niro's personal response to winning the award, he replied with his usual candour: 'Lots of people who win the Oscar don't deserve it, so it makes you a little cynical about what it means. Did it mean anything to me? Well, I don't know. It changes your life like anything will change your life. People react to it. I mean: it's not bad winning it.'

It certainly wasn't for him, as the Oscar opened the doors to Hollywood and beckoned him to enter on its highest level. At thirty-two, the acting career he'd been working on since childhood was now a box-office, Oscar-winning reality.

5 *New Directions*

With his sparkling Oscar on his mantelpiece back in New York, and a desk top covered with scripts, De Niro reviewed his options. He wanted a change of pace and, looking back, he could see he'd done nothing funny on screen since *The Gang That Couldn't Shoot Straight*. Why not a real comedy this time? And what better person to write one than Neil Simon, the uncrowned King of Broadway and a Hollywood prince by any standards? And to direct him in this new script, why not Mike Nichols? As to the plot, why not something De Niro knew well – the life of an unemployed actor?

All these elements came quickly together thanks to Simon's screenplay *Bogart Slept Here*, its title referring to the old Hollywood hotel where the hero spends much of his time. Mike Nichols was excited at the prospect of directing the town's hottest new star, and the project seemed to have all the right ingredients to display Bobby's talents in a new and humorous light. Unfortunately, the ingredients didn't mix well together.

At first reading, Simon's romantic comedy seemed just right for all concerned, in its tale of a struggling actor who is forced to share an apartment with a young mother and her child. When the film went into production, there were major two-page ads in the trade papers heralding the event, with a whimsical drawing of De Niro walking near the venerable Château Marmont Hotel in West Hollywood. Long a stopping-place for the famous and infamous, the hotel would ironically be the setting, in 1982, of John Belushi's drug overdose. The dead star was a close friend of De Niro's.

On paper, *Bogart Slept Here* looked just right, but reports from the set shortly proved it was anything but.

Nichols, the former stand-up comedian turned Oscar-winning movie-director, was a perfectionist who liked giving directions and having them quickly understood and obeyed. Unlike Coppola, he knew exactly what he wanted from an actor and didn't need a lot of talking about it. This was not the way De Niro worked and, with the picture barely before the cameras, rumours began abounding that the film was in deep trouble, and the buzz described an on-the-set battle of wills.

Finally, after several weeks of shooting and a great deal of money spent, the film was shut down and Nichols explained in a newspaper article that his star was just not coming across as funny. The film that was shot early in 1975 will probably never be seen but it's a cinch that, even had it been completed, De Niro would not have given Nichols, as he had Coppola, one of his father's paintings 'as one artist to another'. Instead the plug was pulled, De Niro signed to do a massive film in Italy, and several years later the Simon script was dusted off, repolished and turned into *The Goodbye Girl* – for which Richard Dreyfuss won an Academy Award.

If De Niro was looking for a fast and easy movie shoot, he certainly didn't find it in Italy, where he was to star in Bernardo Bertolucci's historical pageant, *1900*. Two plusses were his Italian heritage and an opportunity to explore it further, as well as the fact that it was to Bertolucci to whom Brando had turned to consolidate his *Godfather* success with the steamily erotic *Last Tango in Paris*. What Bobby had no way of knowing was that European film-making, and Bertolucci's in particular, was a process very different from the ways of Hollywood. He quickly found that out.

Rome welcomed him as a star, and he was given top billing in a cast that included Orson Welles, France's sensational Gerard Depardieu, Dominique Sanda, Sterling Hayden, Donald Sutherland and *Last Tango*'s female star, Maria Schneider. Bertolucci was another story, though. Like Nichols before him, Bertolucci was a perfectionist who preferred 'instructing' his actors rather than allowing them to participate in character improvisation. Happily he understood his young star and was willing to bend the rules a bit, which helped not only De Niro but the film as well.

Bertolucci's vision for *1900* was that it be a sweeping tapestry of Italian history as that country entered the new century and went through its internal convulsions of Socialism, Fascism and the old land-owning aristocracy until the end of World War II. It was a gigantic story seen through many eyes but specifically those of Alfredo and Olmo, two boys born of the century who grew to be best friends, though one was an aristocrat (De Niro) and one a peasant (Depardieu). It was to be Bertolucci's personal version of his country's political upheavals and evolution, and he wanted all the actors to follow him docilely in this great adventure.

Personalities were quick to clash, and the first victim was Orson Welles. In short he'd been replaced by Burt Lancaster, who had earned grudging critical respect when he played a Sicilian nobleman in 1963's *The Leopard*. Then Maria Schneider, Bertolucci's discovery for *Last Tango...*, who had since then undergone an emotional breakdown, began accusing the director of exploiting her sexy image and walked off the picture. She too was replaced, and production began in earnest in early summer 1974 at Rome's sprawling Cinecittà studios.

During the weeks of preparation for his role as the aristocrat, De Niro had come to know and appreciate his opposite number, Gerard Depardieu. In him he saw a kindred spirit – in fact, they were almost each other's national counterparts. In France, Depardieu was a rising star who combined sex-appeal and serious talent. Unlike many other French stars, such as Alain Delon, who was always typecast in his youth because of his beauty, Gerard was offered many types of roles and usually took them. His looks apart, his demeanour made him a believable actor whether playing a peasant or a prince. He was a maverick much like De Niro himself and, as friends, they both anticipated doing their best work.

And the two attempted just that, especially De Niro. When Bertolucci 'instructed', he listened quietly and then carefully interjected his own opinions and suggestions. It was necessary for him, as he told Paul Gardner, because, 'I have to be able to talk to my director. I must know what he thinks, or we shouldn't be working together.'

One scene he felt needed clarification was when he and Depardieu were both supposed to have sex with an epileptic laundress in the back of her sweatshop. The dual sex scene is cut short when the girl has a fit, with Depardieu's character trying to help her while De Niro's just wants to get dressed and out of there; their individual reactions help clarify the personalities. But then Bertolucci wanted to cut it down to just De Niro and the girl, thereby undercutting the scene. De Niro questioned this decision so intensely that Bertolucci changed his mind, and the scene went as originally written. To his credit, Bertolucci was quickly coming to understand his star and, cocking his trademark fedora, listened and accepted his suggestions.

Despite good intentions, 1900 nevertheless quickly ran over its intended shooting schedule, due to constant tinkering and rewriting of the script. Concurrently it also ran well over budget, and for a time it seemed the film would never be finished as months meandered expensively by. Paramount had bargained for a film three hours and fifteen minutes in length but the way Bertolucci was reloading cameras it promised to be much longer. He tried explaining the constant script alterations, stating that, 'Reality in front of the camera is more important than anything. If an actor has been drinking and looks pale (for example), then I use it. I know, it is an expensive kind of documentary for me. And often, I have no idea how to continue a sequence. But that is my technique.' As he'd already been working on the script for two years, he didn't seem in any hurry to perfect his 'technique' and complete the film.

De Niro was right in thinking that his character of Alfredo '...was such an observer that it was difficult to fill him in', but he did his best to interpret Bertolucci's vision. When either the director or the star was not pleased with results, they did it again and again.

Bertolucci had searched for months to get just the right extra players who would look their roles as work-worn peasants, but while realism was essential to him, practicality was not. On seeing the film, it's easy to appreciate the value of the many character extras who indeed give it an earthy power, providing it with the necessary background of realism that Bertolucci relished. He wanted to keep them all in the film – along with almost every other scene – and what resulted has come to be known as Italy's *Heaven's Gate*, an enormously costly exercise in perfectionism which looked beautiful on the screen but not so pretty at the box-office.

Finally it was finished, or at least the shooting of it, and the tab came to a whopping $9 million and enough footage for several movies! Bertolucci spent almost a year editing his masterpiece and, once finished, this labour of love ran some five hours and twenty minutes in length; unmarketable in America.

Naturally his Stateside backers were unhappy, and the film began a back-and-forth history of editing and re-editing that eventually brought its time down to just over four hours.*

One of the film's most titillating aspects was that moviegoers got to see both De Niro and Depardieu in the buff, but was that a valid reason to give up four hours of one's time? And for that matter, one got to see practically every star in the film in a sexual position at one time or another. Lancaster, as an ageing aristocrat, gets to feel up a peasant girl, Sutherland rapes and then kills a young boy, and Dominique Sanda drops her costumes in several scenes.

Though it was gorgeously filmed, reviewers found 1900's theatrics overblown and its story of political upheaval hard to follow. It seemed that the longer the film, the less appealing it was as a moneymaker. De Niro did not escape from it all unscathed. His Alfredo was the unwilling catalyst of much of the action but, while that was logical on the screen, it was not what reviewers expected from the white-hot star who'd just nobly filled Marlon Brando's shoes in *The Godfather Part II*. True, it's difficult to forget De Niro's young godfather but the actor himself knew that a lasting career needs to be built on a variety of memorable roles, and when one finishes watching 1900, one doesn't forget Bobby De Niro.

Although 1900 has been referred to as both Italy's *Heaven's Gate* and its *Gone With the Wind*, until recently few understood why. Paramount accepted and released the four-hour-five-minute version but found few takers. As of March 1988, the film had grossed less than $1 million in the United States. Then Bertolucci's *The Last Emperor* swept the 1987 Academy Awards by winning nine golden statuettes, including Best Picture and Best Director. Paramount sensed a renewed interest not only in Bertolucci but also in 1900, which had shown consistent strength in revival theatres. Now they decided to package the film on video-cassette – the 4½-hour released version – and send it out to stores in a two-cassette package.

By the time of 1900's official theatrical release, De Niro was long gone from old Italy and was immersed in living the reality of 'new' New York. He was getting ready to make a film based

---

* In Europe the film was released at its original length in two parts – but, while it attracted an audience for Part One, few people bothered to turn up for the two-hour finale.

on a script that Brian De Palma had sent him while he was in Italy, one that had intrigued him enormously.

De Niro was anxious to keep his friendships viable, and he and De Palma kept in close touch, always looking for another project to do together, but even though De Palma was not involved in this new venture, he'd nonetheless heartily forwarded it to his friend. Said De Palma, 'It was the strongest stuff I had ever read. I didn't think the movie would ever be made. But if anybody could do it, it would be Bobby.'

Martin Scorsese was set to direct this story of an ex-Marine, a loner who lives in a structureless lifestyle fuelled by junk food and bourbon. An insomniac who can't even find the peace of a good night's sleep, he takes a job driving New York streets at night to fill in the empty hours of his existence. In short, he becomes a *Taxi Driver*.

6 'Are You Talking to Me?'

While *1900* lumbered along in Italy, Martin Scorsese was pacing the floor in Hollywood. Bobby had enthusiastically agreed to star in his new movie, but there was little Marty could do but gnash his teeth until he got back home. 'I can't do it without Bobby,' he mumbled to a friend as he walked anxiously around his small apartment, its walls lined with posters of favourite films. 'I gotta have him.' The reason for this was that De Niro had become part of the deal, and Marty couldn't – and wouldn't – proceed without him. The bond of their similar childhoods was stronger than ever, and this story would delve deeply into the collective mind of their own hometown.

The script for *Taxi Driver* lay on his cluttered coffee table, its red cover practically pulsating with the life contained in its pages, a life defined in terms of desperation, alienation, violence and a bizarre sense of redemption. It contained all these elements because it had been written from the experienced heart by Paul Schrader.

Schrader was a writer who, at the time, was best known for the Robert Mitchum drama about the Japanese Mafia called *The Yakuza*. While not a big hit, the film was successful enough that his subsequent screenplays were guaranteed a serious look by producers – no mean feat in a town that hinged more on box-office than honesty, which *Mean Streets* certainly was. Schrader knew the underbelly of his character, Travis Bickle, from his own lonely, porn-addicted, pill-popping nights. Many of the steps Travis would take on the screen, Schrader had already taken in real life.

Later in his career, Schrader would explore other avenues of darkness, via such unorthodox screenplays as *Cat People* and *American Gigolo* and, like those future works, *Taxi Driver* was also fraught with the off-beat sexuality of its anti-social 'hero' through whose eyes the story is told. Laced with street obscenities, it was obviously a script requiring careful handling.

Scorsese was a director who could tap aspects of Bobby's sexuality as no other director had. In *Mean Streets* Johnny Boy is happily at home grabbing his crotch and strutting when the uptown girls come slumming to his neighourhood bar. He knows what they're looking for and is delighted at the prospect of giving it to them. In *Taxi Driver* Scorsese would scratch the other side of the sexual coin to reveal a painfully shy man very much aware of his masculinity but unable to find a comforting place to put it.

Producers Julia and Michael Phillips were intrigued by this strange screenplay and took it to a major studio for financing. That studio took one long look and wanted to sanitize it on the spot. Neil Diamond was then looking to make his film début, and he was screentested for *Taxi Driver*, a move that brings new meaning to the word 'sanitize'. Next the studio decided they had a director/star package for the project: Robert (*Summer of '42*) Mulligan and Jeff Bridges, a cleancut actor who'd recently been in competition with De Niro in the Academy Award race. Schrader took one look at this combo and turned thumbs down.

By chance and luck, he saw *Mean Streets* and then made sure the producers did the same. He was convinced that the combination of De Niro and Scorsese was exactly what he was looking for, and the Phillipses agreed, quickly signing the pair and presenting this new deal to Columbia Pictures, who then agreed to put up the production money.

Once that was set, Scorsese and De Niro went to work, Martin to scout the exact New York locations to best illustrate the story and Bobby to the Motor Vehicle Department for a hack licence so he could actually take a job driving a cab. For two weeks he cruised and worked the streets of the city, checking out his fares for any available insight into his part, 'I am normally a fairly quiet man,' he told a London interviewer, 'but I chatted to my passengers, keeping within the character I was about to play, and I learned a great deal.' Reportedly he was recognized only twice, with one sympathetic passenger innocently asking, 'You're the actor, aren't you? Guess it's hard to find steady work.' De Niro nonetheless enjoyed the experience and was smart enough to appreciate the fact that his privacy would decrease a great deal more if the film was a hit. To say he prized anonymity is an understatement. 'I like walking around without being bothered. I like the rhythm of the streets. I like to fit.'

He fell into Travis Bickle's skin, eating junk food on the run, not sleeping and dropping weight from his already slender frame to achieve the tautly wired look he would have. To try to sense Travis' growing loneliness and isolation, he prowled for hours around a New York zoo, filing away the caged animals' sense of dismay and unhappiness at their forced surroundings.

For his part, Scorsese did just as well, finding some of the sleaziest streets in Manhattan to film on, including some in Little Italy. He wanted a brutal look to his film, as if Travis is caught up in some great grinding machine of a city, and he found and captured that look courageously.*

His search for supporting players was equally thorough, with him leaning in favour of 'New York types' with whom he'd worked before or whom he knew personally. Harvey Keitel, another *Mean Streets* graduate, came on board to play an evil pimp who sells Jodie Foster's twelve-year-old charms on the street. (Jodie Foster was actually all of thirteen at the time, and the spectre of *Taxi Driver* would haunt her for years. When US President Ronald Reagan was nearly assassinated in 1981, the alleged gunman was an obsessed fan of Jodie Foster and of the film.) Cybill Shepherd was assigned the part of Betsy, the perfect blonde whom Travis falls for, only to lose her interest when he takes her to a pornographic cinema. Peter Boyle was to play a cabby acquaintance of Travis' (the movie was quick to point out that Travis had no real friends), and Albert Brooks was to appear as Betsy's buttoned-up boyfriend.

It was a stunning cast which also included Scorsese himself as a passenger with revenge on his mind.

But Scorsese was interested in the minor parts as well as the showy ones and wanted believably fresh faces whenever possible. For one establishing sequence when Travis goes to a porno theatre and buys one of every stale treat on the shelves, he hired a beautiful young black actress to play the girl behind the counter. Her name was Diahnne Abbott, and she'd been

---

* Interestingly, Scorsese chose to cloak the growing violence and alienation of his film with a sweepingly romantic score by Bernard Herrmann. Herrmann, who had provided classic movie themes for *Citizen Kane*, *North By Northwest* and (prophetically?) *Psycho*, died before the film was released, never knowing that his last movie music was nominated for an Academy Award.

Bobby De Niro's girlfriend for several years. The divorced mother of a young girl, Diahnne had met Bobby when he was first starting out ('I thought he was marvellous but I never expected him to be a star') and was delighted when Scorsese cast her on what loomed as being the most controversial picture of the year. Honest and straightforward, she got the part on her own and brought to it the kind of down-to-earth intensity that was obviously attractive to De Niro. By the time the film was finished, they were more committed to each other than ever.

Diahnne and Bobby's one big scene was an exercise in improvisation as he mumbled over the stale popcorn, crusty candy bars and flat soda pop, yet it worked beautifully. Scorsese, of all people, knew and appreciated his need for improvisation and in several scenes let him do it. The most remembered example of this from *Taxi Driver* comes when Travis, driven to the brink of psychosis, buys a small arsenal of weapons and practises his draw, standing bare-chested in front of a grimy mirror in his slummy apartment. As he snaps the guns in and out of his holsters, he carries on a one-sided conversation with an imaginary opponent. 'Are you talking to me?' he asks insistently three times. 'Well, you must be because I'm the only one here.' Perhaps the most chilling moment of the film, it's easily the one most imitated.

By this point Travis Bickle is beginning to see himself as some kind of urban avenger, willing to stand up to the scum of the city that he sees every night in the back of his cab. What he doesn't realize is that he's slowly slipping over the edge of sanity.

Suprisingly De Niro's acute isolation and growing violence make the viewer almost sympathetic towards him as the bloody finale grows closer. Through his understanding of the complexities and disappointments of Travis, he has made the character understandable; you're almost guiltily cheering him on when he murders the street pimp, just as one would cheer on any hero who conquers the villain for the lady's honour. Audiences understood Travis' bloody rampage and, while stunned by it, were on his side. It took an actor of amazing talent to pull this frightening character off, but De Niro did it. In fact, he'd wanted to accept this acting challenge so badly that he'd turned down a part in the star-crammed *A Bridge Too Far* – and the accompanying paycheque of $500,000 – to make his Travis a screen reality. His salary for *Taxi Driver* was only $35,000, but it was worth it. (His low salary coincided with the meagre $1.3 million budget that was necessary to get Columbia interested and the picture made.)

Reviewers of *Taxi Driver* left a numbed trail behind them as they stumbled out of screening rooms across the country, but underneath the shock was the knowledge that they had just seen a classic, certainly one of the meanest films of the decade but also one of the most unforgettable. Before their collective eyes they'd seen De Niro turn into a messenger from Hell, one of those people who jump out of the darkness of their lives to make blazing headlines. He was able to make his body and mind forge the essence of urban horror, a stranger in a crowd who is really a walking hand-grenade with a loose pin – just about any kind of shock could make him explode. One critic said that Travis Bickle was enough to make him move out of New York in search of calmer pastures, but most were just in sheer awe of the extraordinary skill that went into creating him.

Being an actor eager to take chances had paid off once again for De Niro, and when the critical dust had settled, the box-office returns were over $12.5 million. *Taxi Driver* – love it or hate it – was a huge success, and Bobby had his first name-above-the-title hit. That was only the beginning. He was elated when he was voted Best Actor by the New York Film Critics Circle and picked up the award with Diahnne by his side.

But couldn't he help but wonder what the Motion Picture Academy was thinking? If he was, the question was answered in early February 1977, when the list of Oscar nominees was announced. *Taxi Driver* received four nominations: for Best Picture, Best Supporting Actress (Jodie Foster), Best Musical Score (the recently deceased Bernard Herrmann's stylish score) and Best Actor – Robert De Niro.

The awards were presented on 28 March. Outside in the early evening sunlight, the bleachers were packed with fans, many of whom had camped out overnight just to see the stars make their entrances. One after another they paraded in: Sissy Spacek (a nominee for *Carrie*), Jimmy and Gloria Stewart, Mr and Mrs Kirk Douglas and son Michael, plus dozens more in made-to-order finery, each of them receiving a rousing welcome from the sun-baked fans.

The biggest ovation of all came when a block-long white

limousine deposited Sylvester Stallone and entourage at the edge of the red carpet that swept up to the pillared entrance of the Dorothy Chandler Pavilion. The crowd went crazy, banners appeared with 'GO ROCKY' scrawled across them, and pandemonium reigned. Stallone's *Rocky* had been the surprise hit of the year and, judging from the crowd, his Oscar nomination seemed to be a sure winner. There were no banners for *Taxi Driver*.

Inside the elaborate auditorium the ceremonies unfolded. Any thoughts of a *Taxi Driver* landslide were quickly dashed when Jodie Foster lost to *Network*'s Beatrice Straight, followed by Bernard Herrmann's losing to Jerry Goldsmith's score for *The Omen*. Finally the Best Actor category was announced.

Besides De Niro and Stallone, the nominees included Giancarlo Giannini for *Seven Beauties*, the recently deceased Peter Finch for *Network*, and William Holden, also for that picture. The buzz in the Pavilion's elaborate press room, from *The Hollywood Reporter*'s Richard Hack to everyone's Rona Barrett, had Stallone crowned the latest King of Hollywood while De Niro was labelled a long shot in the Oscar sweepstakes. All bets were called, though, when the award for Best Actor was announced – and Peter Finch's widow came up to the podium to accept it for her late husband.

De Niro was already working on *New York, New York* by then, so he didn't see the Best Picture nod go to *Rocky*. Since finishing *Taxi Driver* and starting the new film, he'd had a uniquely busy year.

His relationship with Diahnne was growing, and he'd long accepted her first marriage and her eight-year-old daughter, Drina. He was crazy about the little girl, and as his relationship grew with her mother, he began to realize how much he'd like to be a father. Diahnne's ambitions as an actress now took second place to Bobby, and the pair formed an easy alliance of friendship and love. At thirty-three, three years older than Diahnne, he suddenly felt the need to plant some roots.

After completing *Taxi Driver*, he immediately signed to star in *The Last Tycoon*, and to get into the title role of the ill and reclusive Hollywood mogul of the thirties, he moved into a rambling Bel-Air mansion where he could soak up the atmosphere of Power Hollywood and shed the uneasy skin of Travis Bickle. It was a tricky time emotionally but Diahnne's patience and understanding of his need for privacy helped bond them even closer.

Bobby was enthusiastic about this new project, despite knowing that it had come to him third-hand. Dustin Hoffman had been offered it but was too busy to do it, and his old friend Al Pacino was next. Pacino, through a lengthy silence, made it clear he wasn't interested.

For long hours Bobby would disappear, later to say he'd spent them walking the silent streets of Paramount Pictures' backlot where the film was to be made. Much later he told an interviewer the secret of the character's motivation: 'I spent time just walking around the studio dressed in these three-piece suits, thinking "This is all mine." '

Finding the essence of Monroe Stahr (the name of the *Last Tycoon*) took him on a different path from his earlier adventures of having to cruise Times Square at midnight looking for a fare. This film gave him an open invitation to revel and luxuriate in the era of Hollywood now remembered as its Golden Age. Instead of travelling back in time to rocky Sicilian villages as he had for *The Godfather Part II* and *1900*, he could stop his internal time-machine at this most glamorous period, Hollywood in the mid-thirties – with himself cast as one of its most important rulers. His Little Italy background would be of no help in Beverly Hills, so he simply turned the situation around and made Beverly Hills work for him.

The Last Tycoon was a novella by F. Scott Fitzgerald which was uncompleted when he died suddenly in 1940 and had tantalized Hollywood ever since. Rumoured to be loosely based on the life of Irving Thalberg, MGM's boy-wonder producer in the early thirties who died of a heart attack at the age of thirty-seven, it really chronicles Fitzgerald's own disillusion and disappointment in this story of a movie studio head who cannot get the girl of his dreams. A simple enough theme certainly, but one which Fitzgerald ably used to evoke all the little losses in Hollywood, from stars and starmakers down to the grips on the lot and the waitresses in the cafeteria.

Producer Sam Spiegel, a money-spender of the Old Guard as well as a money-spinner via such films as *The Bridge on the River Kwai* (1957) and *Lawrence of Arabia* (1962) among many others, wanted to make a film about Hollywood in the thirties, and when he couldn't develop a script he liked, optioned

Fitzgerald's book instead.

While the script was being written, Spiegel went ahead and signed on one of the most talented directors ever to hit Hollywood, Elia Kazan, the man who'd directed Spiegel's 1954 Oscar-winning *On the Waterfront* – the film that won Marlon Brando his first Academy Award. Kazan's mystique among serious actors had elevated him to a position resembling sainthood as an innovative yet sensitive director.

One of the reasons for Kazan's insight was that he'd worked both sides of the fence. During the thirties he had co-starred on Broadway in such plays as 1931's *Men in White* and 1939's *The Gentle People*, opposite Sylvia Sidney, before going on to guide five Pulitzer Prize-winning plays to major success, including any actor's favourite, the classic *Death of a Salesman*. His movie career was sporadic, as he preferred the challenge of sensitive material – anti-Semitism in *Gentleman's Agreement* and racism in *Pinky*, to name but two. Also, and this was of great interest to Bobby, Kazan had directed three of his childhood favourites: Brando, James Dean and Montgomery Clift. From Brando he had elicited two of his strongest performances – as Stanley in *A Streetcar Named Desire* and as the Mexican revolutionary Emilio Zapata in *Viva Zapata*, while from Dean he'd drawn the magic that had made *East of Eden* such an enduring classic. Unfortunately the combination of Kazan and Clift came too late in that star's career to do either much good. By 1960, when they made *Wild River*, Clift was but a shadow of the screen god he'd been a scant ten years before, and Kazan was barely able to get any kind of performance out of him, let alone a great one.

Sixteen years later, though, the situation seemed oddly reversed. Kazan had a hot young star to work with in a big-budget picture but would find no pay-off. The late Vivien Leigh once described Kazan as a man 'who sends his suit out to be cleaned and rumpled', alluding to his habit of putting his work first. By this time, though, much of his concentrated genius seemed used up. *The Last Tycoon* was the last time Kazan sat in the movie-director's chair.

One thing the film definitely had on its side was its actors, all of whom brought their own perspectives to the story of Hollywood and its always-changing cast of characters.

As Monroe Stahr, Bobby appears very thin and gaunt as the ailing head of mythical International-World Studios. (In his memoirs Kazan says that he lost forty-two pounds to get that look.) When we first meet him, Stahr is the recent widower of a great movie queen whose memory he reveres. Then, during a freak accident in which a soundstage is flooded, a golden idol floats across his vision, and his eyes rivet on one of the girls cradled on the water-born Buddha – a girl who is the image of his dead wife. Immediately taken, he sets out to find and pursue her while all around him buzz the inner workings of a major studio of its time, like a beehive full of restless inhabitants all anxious to make an impression.

Fifties teen idol Tony Curtis pops up as an ageing Latin Lover who's losing not only his fans but his hair as well. Jack Nicholson, fresh from his triumph in *One Flew Over the Cuckoo's Nest*, appears as a union official who precipitates Stahr's breakdown, while Robert Mitchum slouches through the role of a studio executive.

The first woman in Stahr's life was played by newcomer Theresa Russell as Cecilia, who's quickly forgotten once he sets eyes on Kathleen Moore, brought to screen life by another newcomer, Ingrid Boulting. She had met Spiegel through a dinner-party acquaintance, and he in turn introduced her to Kazan. With her pert beauty and bright personality, Kazan agreed to screen test her, and the determined *ingénue* got the part. 'I felt like working,' she later said, 'and I knew I could play Kathleen.' Beautiful she was; an actress is another question. That question wasn't asked about Russell, a strikingly good performer who brought a vivid intensity to her screen début as the girl after Stahr's broken heart. Now married to director Nicolas Roeg, she recently won critical applause in *Black Widow*.

Kazan took his company of actors and proceeded to shoot the film as if it were a Garbo picture of forty years before. The set was completely off limits to visitors, and publicity kept at an absolute minimum. Producer Spiegel heartily agreed with this approach, remembering well the publicity overkill of *The Great Gatsby* just a few years before – another lavish story of a man with power and money, which sank at the box-office despite numerous magazine covers.

De Niro couldn't have been more pleased with this edict, and Kazan was impressed with him. 'He's the only actor I've ever known who called me up on Friday night after we got through shooting and said, "Let's work tomorrow and Sunday together." He's the hardest working actor I've ever met and one of the best guys I've ever met in the business ... He finds release and fulfilment in becoming other people. Picture after picture he gets deep into the thing. He's found his solution for living at a time like this in his work.'

The Last Tycoon was an ambitious attempt at answering the question, 'What goes wrong with Hollywood lives?' and De Niro succeeded ably at showing off his latest creation as he glided daily between a sumptuous rented house and the studio where he was temporarily king. If anything, the film proved that, even at the top of the Hollywood heap, there are as many frustrations and disappointments as we all face and that life is not an easy ride for anyone.

While De Niro had found himself in his work, he was also able to accept that it could be more than that, and it was only a short time before his closest pals were let in on his and Diahnne's plans to marry.

7   Marriage and Music

After *Taxi Driver* and *The Last Tycoon*, De Niro's screen image was desperately in need of a change. The public had embraced him – if at arm's length – in the former and rejected his sensitive Monroe Stahr, which led many to believe that, as Sly Stallone would quickly find out when he tried to break his *Rocky* mould, the public only wanted to see him as an angry outsider and preferably a member of a gang.

Ironically it was Martin Scorsese, of all people, who came up with the idea for a change of pace – and what bigger one than a great Hollywood musical with a multi-million-dollar budget? It was to be, once again, a personal challenge for Scorsese, just as *Mean Streets* and *Taxi Driver* had been, only this time he was exploring the Golden Era of the Movie Musical and wanted Bobby to ride along beside him all the way to *New York, New York*.

However, before Bobby could commit himself to a new film, there was a very personal affair to be attended to, and that was his relationship with Diahnne.

So secret and quietly kept were Bobby and Di's living-arrangements that many friends didn't know she had already been living with him for some time. When they found out, many thought that he had purposely kept the relationship quiet to hide the fact that he was involved with a black woman. Marie Brenner asked Harvey Keitel if that was the case, only to have him reply, 'Are you kidding? If you asked Bobby that, he'd say something like, "Is Di black?" '

Just the same, when Di and De Niro decided to get married, in June 1976, it was a very quiet affair to which reporters were decidedly not invited. Instead he felt it was a time to share only with those closest to him, not only the friends who'd seen him through the tough early days of his career but also those who had helped it develop as brilliantly as it had so far.

The non-denominational ceremony was performed at New York's Ethical Culture Society, and the guest list reflected much of Bobby's career. From his early theatre days came Julie Bovasso, producer Joseph Papp and Sally Kirkland, while his early movies were represented by John Hancock, who'd directed him in *Bang the Drum Slowly*. Shelley Winters was there as well, with other friends including Jay Cocks and Verna Fields, Barry Primus, with whom he'd shortly be acting in *New York, New York*, Harvey Keitel and Martin Scorsese. When Marie Brenner later asked guest Paul Schrader about those in attendance, he replied, 'Everybody there was somebody who had helped Bobby to become a different person.' Somebody better? asked Marie Brenner. 'Absolutely not – somebody different.'

And that was just what Bobby was about to do again, helped in part by a forthright and wonderfully talented actress.

Up to this point Bobby had never met his female match on screen. In his earlier films women had usually been just the means to a violent end, such as Cybill Shepherd and Jodie Foster in *Taxi Driver* and the assorted beauties of *1900*. But then along came Liza Minelli.

Would that Liza's mother, the late Judy Garland, had had her daughter's strength in dealing with the men in her turbulent life which Liza showed in this film, handling the baddest saxophone player of them all, De Niro's Jimmy Doyle. As Francine Evans,* Liza showed a depth of talent denied her mother, whose real emotions were always clearly visible on screen. At thirty-one she'd already weathered several Hollywood hurricanes and, while she still had personal stormy weather ahead, was then in a sound professional and emotional place – which was good considering the on-screen emotional battering she was about to receive.

Liza had top billing in the picture, and De Niro's Jimmy Doyle made her earn it. Ironically she knew little about him at the time, and her first meeting with director Scorsese was 'not a good omen'. She said to him, 'It's going to be really interesting doing this film. Especially with James Caan,' Scorsese took a deep breath and corrected her. 'It got worse as it went along,' he later told. 'I asked her if she'd seen *Mean Streets*, I reminded her De

---

* At one point Barbra Streisand was talked about as Francine Evans opposite a Jimmy Doyle played by Ryan O'Neal.

Niro was in that, and she said: "Is he the guy with the suit all the time?" ' That, of course, was Harvey Keitel.

The film opens on VJ-Day 1945, the war is finally over, the soldiers, both male and female, are home and it's party-time in Times Square. De Niro starts off his festivities by tossing his uniform out of his hotel window, donning white slacks and a shirt emblazoned with the Statue of Liberty and then setting off to find a bedmate. When he meets Francine in a crowded ballroom filled with jitterbugging military like himself, there's an immediate sexual chemistry between them, he the over-cocky seducer and she the reluctant object of his desire. She tries to tell him no nicely, but Jimmy Doyle won't give up and begins to show an annoying machismo as he subsequently pursues her all over New York. From her background as a band singer, Francine knows men and fends him off – at least temporarily – while, as an actress, Liza matches her co-star in screen power and gives as good as she gets. Yet even Liza/Francine has her limits, and her resolve wears down when he shows up at a club where she's appearing. After a marriage proposal that includes De Niro's lying down in front of a taxicab to keep her from leaving, she finally accepts his offbeat approach and they leave in it together to find a Justice of the Peace.

Naturally the marriage is rocky from the beginning; they have a little boy, they fight, she sings, they fight, he plays the sax and forms his own band, they fight – back and forth until she takes up a movie offer and leaves him for Hollywood and stardom. He finally has a success with his own club and with a new singer played by Diahnne Abbott, who sings a sexy rendition of 'Honeysuckle Rose'.

When Francine returns to Manhattan as a big movie star, she gives a concert and sings a version of Jimmy's jazzy theme song, now called 'New York, New York'. She makes a blazingly successful return to the city, and Jimmy sees, first-hand, what a complete woman she's become. Finally as equals they meet in Francine's dressing-room and talk over old times and a possible future. After saying hello to his now six-year-old son, Jimmy leaves, shortly calling Francine back to ask her out for Chinese food. It's a simple request and one eagerly accepted, harking back, as it does, to the early days and the scramble for success. He says he'll meet her at the stage door.

Jimmy shows up, nervously anticipating this reunion, while, inside, Francine is doing exactly the same thing. Across their faces flash looks of affection, love and resignation as they realize that what might lie ahead – if they let it – will be every bit as painful as what's been left behind. Francine exits by a side door while Jimmy eventually walks off alone in the city rain, but now sure that the past is best being just that. It's the most compelling and, oddly, the most romantic scene in the picture and certainly a far cry from the 'happy endings' of traditional Hollywood musicals. (Ironically, again, 'Happy Endings' was the name of a gigantic production number heralding Francine's Hollywood success that was cut from the release print of the film.)

But then *New York, New York* never started out to be a return to MGM's musically golden days when Liza's mother was queen of the lot but instead was Scorsese's interpretation of that genre – and his ideas of anything seldom ended up in smiles.

Scorsese frankly said that the picture was primarily about '...the period in your life when you're about to make it; you know you're talented, you know you're this, you know you're that, but you just don't quite make it, not for another four or five years'. It's that time in your life, he says, '...when your first marriage breaks up; when people who are crazy in love with each other can't live with each other'. It's this interchange of confused relationships that forms the plot of *New York, New York*, necessarily making it sing a few high notes of ecstasy between many that sound like the tortured whine of an amateur accordian player. Despite the fact that it was publicized as an $8 million movie musical, it was far from being rosy close-ups and flashing teeth.

Certainly De Niro didn't have much time for smiling while preparing for the part. Pucker up? Yes. But smile? Another story. For research into the art of playing the saxophone he went right to the top of the field, contacting Georgie Auld to tutor him in the finer points of the instrument, subsequently spending many hours with him in doing so. Those long hours paid off, making him look like a professional musician in the film – which is exactly why he'd done it. To *American Film* magazine he explained that, 'It was just to learn it so that I wouldn't look as if I didn't know what I was doing. I really worked on it very hard. But I wonder if I should have saved a little more energy for other things and just worried about what was going to be seen. I worked like hell on that thing. But you either have to know it so well that you can really do it or you have to find a way to do it so that you can know just enough and still feel comfortable with it.'

While directors might be pleased and audiences astounded by De Niro's dedication, occasionally his teachers found it debilitating. Georgie Auld was one. An expert whom De Niro highly respected, Auld entered into three months of intense study with the actor, and hardly an hour went by when Bobby didn't feel the need for more information. 'He asked me ten million questions a day,' Auld said later. 'He got to be a pain in the ass.'

Bobby's only defence for this was his innate need for perfection. 'It's my job as an actor to create the feeling that I'm the one doing the playing. I've seen too many movies where the actor is moving his fingers one way and the music is going in the opposite direction up the scale. Who wants that?' Certainly not him. It was rumoured that he took the role in the picture not necessarily because of either Scorsese or Minelli but because he wanted a good reason to learn a musical instrument, in this case the tenor sax!

To get it right, a pain in the ass he might have been but the combination of De Niro and Minelli brought out the best of each. From the shy and awkward teenager who studied at the Herbert Berghof Acting School in Greenwich Village in the early sixties, Liza Minelli had blossomed into an Oscar-winning star who'd gained added respect by winning an Emmy and a Tony as well. Her Oscar, for 1972's *Cabaret*, seemed to presage a major film career, but since then she'd had two disappointments, the gossip-ridden *Lucky Lady* followed in that same year, 1976, by *A Matter of Time*, her father, Vincente Minelli's movie swansong which she had filmed in Paris opposite Ingrid Bergman.

Both stars needed a mainstream audience-pleaser, and *New York, New York* seemed just the ticket. The ride turned out a bit uneven and bumpy at times but one never less than interesting.

On the MGM lot where the picture was to be made the two stars were allowed to wallow in legends. Liza had a soundstage dressing-room that her mother had used when she was the musical queen of the lot – she recognized the chandelier in stunned amazement when she first entered the suite. Meanwhile De Niro was practising the saxophone and his lines not far away in Greta Garbo's former quarters, a suitable choice with his penchant for privacy so intense that newspapers were calling him 'the male Garbo'.

Liza's strongly individual screen presence had been able to make weak men strong (Michael York in *Cabaret*, for example) but now she was being asked to tackle the screen's toughest guy. She decided to do it the old-fashioned way – with sex-appeal. From the moment we meet her in a crowded victory ballroom, still wearing her WAC uniform, she exudes a brightly optimistic sexuality whose sparkle is only briefly dampened by the onslaught of Jimmy Doyle. It was a most demanding part for her, and she later said of the hectic pace of the movie, 'I don't know how any of us survived it. It was like a whirlwind – it's the only film where I can't remember sitting down.' Perhaps it was the momentum of Liza's character (and her own personality) that helped her through Scorsese's reconstructed forties funhouse but she was able to hold her own opposite her volatile co-star.

Volatile onscreen anyway, as Bobby was still keeping his private life as quiet as possible. Most moviegoers, in fact, didn't realize that the stunning black singer in the film was his wife, as in public pictures she was usually out of camera range. As a couple they lived as quietly as possible, considering the demands of his stardom, and usually they most enjoyed themselves abroad, particularly in Rome, where he had so many happy memories.

De Niro became a father when he adopted Diahnne's eight-year-old daughter, Drina, and shortly after that Diahnne became pregnant. Their son, Raphael, was born near the end of shooting the picture, and when a reporter questioned Shelley Winters about it, she replied, 'Did you hear about the baby's name? They were staying at the Hotel Raphael in Rome when he was conceived. Raphael. What a sweet, romantic name. I'm glad they weren't staying at the Hilton.'

Though work on *New York, New York* stretched on for months, De Niro was in a happy mood, as usual assuming along the way some of the characteristics of Jimmy Doyle's breezily optimistic outlook. The film looked like a winner, and he was delighted that Scorsese continued to be amenable to his suggestions. One of the spontaneous moments of improvisation he was especially pleased with was when he threw himself in front of the taxi in the 'will-you-marry-me' scene which ultimately proved one of the highlights of the picture. He was also enjoying the experience of working with Liza Minelli.

Liza's several songs – including the now-classic title tune which was written especially for her – were gorgeously photographed, and she never looked or sounded better. This was no accident, as Scorsese's re-creation of the Big Band era had been remarkably researched and highlighted by personal recollections. 'I was born in 1942,' he said. 'I remember the records and films of the forties from my early childhood. I wanted to relate what that music meant to me growing up and connect that with the reality of the film. New York on screen was more real to me than New York itself, even though I lived there!'

Unfortunately Scorsese's enthusiasm ran away with him in the editing room where, once again, the business of making movies overwhelmed artistic considerations. When he'd completed his first cut, the picture ran almost 4½ hours. Predictably the producers were upset, so he cut it down to two hours and twenty-two minutes. United Artists was still unhappy with the length and took the film to get it into a playable length of just over two hours. One huge sacrifice they made in doing that was slicing out the Minelli production number called 'Happy Endings', a lavish Francine-as-movie-star segment that those who saw it have never forgotten, thinking it the true high-point of the film. United Artists put it back in the print for a 1981 reissue but that didn't do much business as, by then, it was regarded as an 'old' movie and few customers showed up. It's absent from the current video-cassette version.

When Liza was out on the talk-show trail selling *Arthur 2* in June 1988, she appeared on *The Oprah Winfrey Show* and, when asked to name her favourite film experience, brought up *New York, New York*, mainly because it had become so provocative over the years. After speaking warmly of her co-star, she added of the film, 'We all thought it was going to be a huge hit – but it wasn't. But the funny thing is that people still watch it and talk about it, and love it. It's the movie that won't die.'

The making of the film did serve at least one purpose, though, and that was giving both the director and his male star a break from their former intensity. Said Scorsese, 'I wanted to have some fun. It's hard to do pictures like *Taxi Driver*, awfully hard. Why should people want to go to the movies and be batted over the head and mugged for two hours? Which in a sense is what happens to you in both *Taxi Driver* and *Mean Streets*. More than anything else, I wanted to have some fun with this film. It's the kind of movie I always wanted to direct.'

It's a good thing the pair had this break, and he and Bobby were already conferring about another project, the screen biography of boxing's notorious bad boy Jake La Motta, to be called *Raging Bull*. Bobby started taking boxing lessons almost immediately, adding a thin sheen of muscle to his 5 foot 10½ inch frame. Before he tested himself in the ring in front of a movie camera, though, he had to face a different kind of challenge – the Vietnam War in a little epic to be called *The Deer Hunter*.

8   Battle Fatigue

By now Hollywood was regarding De Niro's professional statements with a somewhat jaundiced eye, as it was clear he'd turned into a workaholic. After *Taxi Driver*, he'd said, alluding to the fact that *Taxi*, *The Last Tycoon* and *1900* had been made in quick succession, 'I really didn't plan to have so many films in a row with no breaks. I didn't plan to do that, but I wanted to do this work. In the future, I will keep more time between pictures.' Once shooting on *New York, New York* was completed it was the same story again when he announced he'd be dropping out for a year to be with his wife and baby son, as well as supervising the building of a new house in Los Angeles' ultra-fashionable Brentwood. He ended up buying one built in the fifties instead* but he barely had time to settle in before getting involved with one of the biggest films of his career.

Producers were beginning to accept that in De Niro they had an actor who could strike like lightning at any time. One of the people who wanted to harness this combustible energy was director Michael Cimino. Now 'famed' as the director of the mega-buck failure (and boring) *Heaven's Gate*, in 1978 he had a better reputation thanks to the success of *Thunderbolt and Lightfoot*, which he'd written and directed.

That had been both a personal statement and a moneymaking hit film but four years had slipped by before he had another film idea. He knew he wanted De Niro to star in this project, *The Deer Hunter*, and he knew just how to attract the actor's attention. 'Michael Cimino,' he told a British reporter, 'sent me the script

---

* De Niro kept this house until August 1987, when it was sold to Lucie Arnaz and her husband, Laurence Luckenbill, for $1,275,000. It was described by estate agents as 'a California contemporary with extensive plants, swimming pools, guest house, sauna and views of the city and ocean'. Shades of *The Last Tycoon* himself!

with a picture of a guy with a deer tied over the hood of a white Cadillac, with steelmills in the background – it was such a great shot. I met Cimino a few times and went with him to look at the locations in America. I was curious and it was a way of getting to know him.'

This six-week odyssey gave Cimino and De Niro a chance to scrutinize the environments and lives of steelworkers, the movie's main characters, and provided private insight into their sorrows, struggles and triumphs. They found many suitable places for possible shooting – and also one of its major characters. During a visit to the US Steel plant in Gary, Indiana, they met a worker who had just the right look and personality for the role of Axel, and he was quickly signed to play this major part.

They went to grimy steel towns spread over West Virginia, Pennsylvania and Ohio, visiting veterans' hospitals and talking to actual prototypes of their story's characters. For De Niro it was an enlightening trip. 'I spent a lot of time in Mingo Junction and Stuebenville, Ohio, soaking up the environment,' he said. 'I talked to the mill workers, drank and ate with them, played pool. I tried to become as close to becoming a steelworker as possible without actually working a shift at the mill. I'd have done that, too, except none of the steel mills would let me do it. They let me visit and watch but not actually get involved. No one recognized me as being an actor during that time. Friends just introduced me as Bob and I went from there.' It seems almost impossible that he wasn't recognized while doing this but, again, the burying of his own personality into the one he was researching proved to be seamless.

At this point in time, 1979, the Vietnam War was still an unpopular subject with millions of Americans, and the producers of such films as *Go Tell the Spartans* and *The Boys In Company C* had found out the hard way that it was box-office poison as well. Cimino had to turn to the British film company EMI for his initial financing, some $7.5 million. EMI saw the validity in Cimino's idea, which was centred on a group of steelworkers in fictional Clairton, Pennsylvania, whose relationships are drastically altered by the war. (EMI showed great faith indeed, since Cimino had no script but only the kernel of one. It was written just before and during production and constantly changed throughout shooting.) Yet while it was based on that premise, Cimino asserted that the film was really 'about ordinary people who go through a crisis and come out of it to continue their lives'.

Roughly divided into three sections, *The Deer Hunter* is about a group of friends before, during and after the war, friends who work together in the mill, socialize at the local beerhall and marry the girls they'd fallen in love with in high school. De Niro's Michael Vronsky is the character who's the linchpin of the group.

The beginning of the film shows them hard at work in what appears a living hell of heat and molten steel. And these were not special-effects images! After weeks of negotiations and the tab for $5 million worth of insurance, Cimino was finally allowed to bring his cast and crew into US Steel's Central Blast Furnace in Cleveland, Ohio. Dubbed 'the Widow-Maker' by the men who'd long toiled there, the site was drastically realistic but worth all the effort, as it brought viewers immediately inside the world of Michael, played by De Niro, and his closest friends.

Stan (played by John Cazale), Steven (John Savage), Nick (Christopher Walken) and Axel (Chuck Aspergren) are first seen wearing asbestos clothing as they work in front of the furnace spewing molten metal at 3,000°. Its heat practically blisters off the screen and perfectly sets the atmosphere for the violence to follow and from which their own reactions and attitudes have been forged. These are obviously men who are used to facing reality on a daily and deadly level.

We get a much more intimate look into their lives when everyone gathers for Steven's wedding, an old-fashioned Slav family affair with bridesmaids in matching pink gowns, men stuffed into obviously rented tuxedoes, and babushkaed mothers overseeing the details. At the reception we meet one of the bride's attendants, Linda, played by Meryl Streep, and while she's ostensibly Nick's girlfriend, we see her obvious attraction to Michael when he finally asks her to dance. The magic between De Niro and filmdom's Ice Princess was immediately apparent, and their stilted, nervous banter is made all the more charming for the underlying emotion. Ironically it's Michael's attraction to his friend's girl that makes us first feel sympathetic towards him.

The De Niro acting style mixed well with Meryl Streep's, with their mutual devotion to the craft apparent. She later told a *Life* magazine reporter, 'When you look into his eyes, it's like looking into the fathomless deep. In my scenes with him I felt the unreality of the set and the cameras and all those things that want to interfere. Bobby's eyes were like – oh! I just felt enveloped in their gaze. Huge emotions right under the surface.'

Meryl was feeling other emotions as well. She'd taken the film primarily because her lover, John Cazale, was one of its stars, playing Stan. Her part was relatively small and not well defined, and Cimino let her contribute to her own dialogue. As she did so, the part expanded, eventually into one worthy of a Supporting Actress nomination next Oscar time. While she was doing it, though, the real reason was that it was happily time-consuming and helped her clear her head from the private hell she was going through – Cazale had bone cancer and was going to die, and this would be their only film together. (He died before its release and never saw the results of her work.) This was the terrifying fact that spurred her on. 'They needed a girl between two guys in the movie and I was it. I was ecstatic to be in it because of John.' When the shooting was delayed for three months, they both wondered if it would ever work out. Then, just before start of production, the film's backers found out about Cazale's health after a routine insurance examination and ordered Cimino to drop him.

'I told him [the company spokesman] he was crazy,' Cimino later remembered. 'I told him we were going to shoot the movie in the morning and that this would wreck the company. I was told that, unless I got rid of John, he would shut down the picture ...' The ensuing battle royal left Cimino limp with frustration and sadness, heightened when EMI told him to write an alternative script which excluded John's character completely. In answer he slammed down the phone. 'I told him that not only was I not going to write an alternate script and he could shut down the film for all I cared.' Realizing what was happening, Meryl decided that if John was fired she would leave too. Then amazingly, EMI backed down and the filming began in earnest.

The resultant chemistry between De Niro and Streep was due largely to their mutal need for absolute honesty in their acting and their uncanny ability to transform their own personalities into what the director wanted. Instead of being a radiant beauty, she was content to make herself look plain, as Linda, the smalltown girl who's waiting for her life to start. Their shared background of stage acting also helped, and De Niro hesitantly came to admire her. When she'd whisk out a blow-dryer to dry off the sweat on her forehead when the set became oppressively hot, he was particularly amused. 'Women who are very beautiful often let their beauty inhibit them. They tend to have no character. When a woman is beautiful and has that extra edge – like Meryl – it's nice ... She was always around getting people to laugh', and the *Deer Hunter* set needed as much spontaneous humour as possible.

After the wedding scenes, the friends go to the mountains for a session of 'male bonding' and shooting deer, and the scene was shot some 10,000 feet above sea level on Mt Baker in Washington – yet another pay-off from the 150,000 miles De Niro and Cimino had travelled in search of the right locations. It's a wild and boozy outing which ends with the thunderclap of a rifle – and an instantaneous scene shift to a South-east Asian battleground.

Michael, Nick and Steven are now plunged in the horror of the war, and the intensity of their plight is quickly made obvious. With his need for realism, Cimino relocated cast and crew to Thailand for the war scenes, using it as a substitute for Vietnam. Still, it was a dangerous place, undergoing its own political turmoils, so that Royal Thai policemen were assigned to protect the unit, one for every three film-crew members.

After their capture by the Viet Cong, the trio are held in a remote jungle prison, and the scenes of their torture and confinement are the film's most brutally convincing ones. Their near-rabid captors imprison them in bamboo cages which are partially submerged in a rat-infested swamp, and they're let out only for their captors' amusement.

The most talked-about scene in the picture comes when they're forced to play Russian Roulette, passing a loaded gun around a table while their tormentors make bets as to which one will blow his brains out first. Steven is wounded, and gradually the players are decimated until only Michael and Nick remain. Nick is almost crazy with fear, and John Savage played the scenes with an eerie sense of believability. When it's his turn again, De Niro's Michael has to talk him into taking it as his last chance for survival. When he puts the gun to his head, there's a collective audience intake of breath, and when the barrel clicks to an empty chamber and he's saved, a whoosh of relief filled theatres.

When at last it's Michael's turn, he takes the gun and manages to turn it on his tormentors and, after retrieving the wounded Steven from his sunken cage, they try to make an escape.

The graphic emotions of the roulette sequences were difficult for the actors to maintain. De Niro later said that it '…was very hard to sustain that kind of intensity. I mean we were really slapping each other; you sort of get worked up into a frenzy … It took a long time.'

Cimino faced equally difficult, if different problems with the escape. In the plot the three are picked up by a helicopter, with Michael and Nick barely able to grab onto it before it ascends in the air. Then the weakened Nick falls off and into the river, with Michael following to save him. It required an elaborate stunt which De Niro and Savage insisted on doing themselves, despite the protests of the professionals in the crew over the danger of the thirty-foot fall into the icy waters of the River Kwai.

Stunt co-ordinator Buddy Van Horn instructed them in how to take their falls, and then the helicopter took off with the two actors hanging onto its skids. Over a two-day period the stars peformed this stunt some fifteen times before getting it right for the cameras – and one time almost killed them. Cimino later told it this way to *Esquire* magazine: 'We were coming in at the bridge. It had been raised a little so the helicopter wouldn't have to fly so low. The two runners slipped under the steel cables that held the bridge. What that meant was that, as soon as the chopper lifted off, it would pull the whole bridge up. The chopper would go down and everybody would be killed.' Savage screamed a warning to the pilot but he didn't understand English, and the helicopter churned to one side, throwing De Niro and Savage with it. Bobby yelled 'Drop!' and they went out the open hatch and down into the muddy river. Thankfully there were motorboats nearby, and they were quickly pulled out of the water. Once the immediate danger was past, the two actors simply charged the experience up to the overall cost of realism that pervaded Cimino's film.

Chris Walken experienced the same sense of commitment, and his respect for De Niro helped convey the sense of total involvement the actors felt for each other. He noted that the feeling of comradeship '...is one of the things that shows in the film, but it had some bearing on the characters. They're supposed to have been friends for twenty years, there's a powerful feeling between them. I think my feelings about his work helped create an impression of warmth and friendship.'

As the war drags on, the three friends are separated, and Michael returns home not knowing the fate of his pals. His thinking has been changed forever by the brutality of his experiences, and when he first sees the 'Welcome Home' banner strung across Clairton's main street, he quietly tells the cab-driver to keep going. While his friends and family are hailing him as a hero, he doesn't believe it – or, rather, knows he's not.

In the bushes near his old home, he waits for Linda to get back from her day at the supermarket, and the pair are uneasily reunited. Looking around his familiar hometown and then at Linda, he mumbles, 'I feel a lot of distance. I feel far away.' Linda, having stayed locked in her private world of daily routine, seems almost to envy even this much emotion as she replied, 'I don't know what I feel.'

Learning that Nick is missing in Vietnam, Michael returns there to find him, only to discover that his childhood friend is now a glassy-eyed stranger in the bars of Saigon. Their one remaining link of communication is Russian Roulette, and Nick insists they play again ... this time he loses.

Steven is finally located in a veteran's hospital, minus his legs, and Michael brings him home for Nick's funeral. In some strange way the friends are back together, and after the ceremony they gather at their favourite bar where, after a few drinks, they sing 'God Bless America'. By now that national anthem has become a requiem as well.

When the public first saw the finished product, early in 1979,* there were wildly mixed reactions. For many the war was still a raw wound, and to have it ripped open again on such a graphic scale resulted in reports of people becoming actually ill while viewing the violent scenes, with grown men bursting into tears

* For Academy Award consideration, it was released in December 1978 in Los Angeles. Cimino knew that to sell the picture to the general public he would need all the help he could get, and any Oscar nominations would only add to its image.

and others running out of the theatre. America was still much divided over the war and its effects, and while *The Deer Hunter* didn't resolve the conflicts of its survivors, it at least made them examine their feelings about it under the microscope of their own lives.

As Cimino had suspected when he created the scene, the Russian Roulette sequence caused the most controversy. Critics called it gratuitously violent, especially since it was a fictional situation with no real basis in fact. Tempers and editorials flared from coast to coast until, finally, an executive of Universal, the distributor of *The Deer Hunter*, was forced to make a statement in defence of the film's content and the way Cimino had chosen to portray the enemy. 'Of course, that specific incident didn't happen. It's a *film*, and films use metaphors.' He could have added that, when necessary, movies also sometimes rewrite history when it helps to move the plot along.

The controversy about the depiction of the Viet Cong didn't dampen De Niro's spirits. He'd been impressed with the dramatic possibilities of the idea from the beginning, and he didn't falter now that it was under fire. In fact, he'd sacrificed personal time to do it, telling one interviewer that, 'I really didn't want to do anything until *Raging Bull* [was ready]. But I liked the story and the dialogue. It was so simple. It seemed so real to me.' When asked about the life-threatening chances taken during the making of the picture, he admitted, 'We were risking our lives. You want it to look authentic, but it is a movie ...'

In Hollywood, however, controversy over a film has always been a natural way to bring attention to it, no matter how unpopular the subject might be, and it certainly didn't hurt *The Deer Hunter*. While there were many people who found fault with the way the story was told, there was no ignoring the fact that it was an important film, worthy of respect, and it quickly became one of the most prestigious, if not the biggest moneymaker (it ultimately grossed $27.4 million).

By now De Niro's name was becoming synonymous with 'important' pictures, and *The Deer Hunter* was made more so when it was showered with Oscar nominations – including one for him in the Best Actor Category. (The film claimed a total of nine nominations, including Meryl Streep for Best Supporting Actress, Christopher Walken for Best Supporting Actor and

Cimino for Best Director. Walken and Cimino walked away winners.)

When Oscar night rolled around in April 1979 De Niro was nowhere to be seen in Los Angeles' Dorothy Chandler Pavilion. Barry Spikings, the film's producer, explained away his absence by saying, 'He said he was terrified and couldn't face the occasion.' In reality he had more personal matters consuming his attention.

His marriage had taken a decided turn for the worse, and Bobby and Diahnne had separated. It was all kept very quiet, as was now his trademark when dealing with private matters, but his friends knew. They also understood that it was a pattern between the couple that would recur often. Said one, 'They break up and then they are together. It's been that way for years ... They just go their own way and see each other when they feel like it.'

Ironically it was De Niro's growing success as an actor that had decided them to wed in the first place. Just after the marriage he was quoted as saying, 'Neither Di nor I would have ever signed the papers knowing there might be all sorts of hard times ahead of us. You can struggle together as man and woman but when you become man and wife the contract creates obligations .... We wanted to have children. We wouldn't have gone ahead and had them without marrying because eventually it places an undue moral burden on them .... I never thought it took particular courage marrying someone who isn't white .... But when I married Diahnne, no one said anything to me about it. There was no warning – as there was to Sammy Davis when he wanted to marry Kim Novak, and he was warned off. If someone thought about it at all, nothing was ever said ... and that's just as well. Because I wouldn't have listened anyway '

In retrospect, that attitude almost mirrored that of the man he was getting ready to depict on the screen. And like that man, he'd find that love, challenges and defeat often come when least expected. It's also very possible that this new project, to be directed by Martin Scorsese, was adding its own distinct pressures. De Niro was preparing both physically and mentally for the part of boxer Jake La Motta in a screen version of the ex-middleweight champion's autobiography *Raging Bull*, and the intensity required was unusually tough. Any relationship was liable to suffer under the punishing regimen of preparation he'd set for himself. Long hours were spent in boxing lessons with La Motta himself, while even more were used to steep himself in the man's pugnacious personality – something Jake's own wife, Vickie, had serious problems handling but which were a major part of the story. De Niro couldn't have been easy to be around and, in fact, stayed in a Los Angeles hotel during the filming while Diahnne was just a few miles away in their Brentwood home.

Nonetheless the separation hurt him deeply, and he tried to explain it to a friend, saying, 'I could have been just as happy without all the fame ... even happier. I would probably have gone on being an ordinary guy, living a simple life and nothing would have changed my marriage. I miss Di and the kids terribly. They are always on my mind. I want to be very close to my children, but because I am working and have to bring in an income, it is impossible for me to be with them.'

9 *Raging Bully*

Any fears about either financial or career security as an actor were obliterated forever in Bobby's case with the success of *Raging Bull*. It placed him firmly on top of the movie heap – but proved to be a long and strenuous climb up that slippery mountain.

He was making top star money at last, but the memories of the early years and his scrambling for paying parts provoked him to make sure it was going in profitable and secure directions. There had been too many 'stars' left in the dust of bankruptcy after a few hit films, and Bob was determined not to be one of them.

Shelley Winters told a *Vanity Fair* writer an anecdote which illustrates both his concern and his *naïveté* about money matters. 'By now we had the same business manager – Jay Julien,' she recalled. 'One day Jay told us he was investing some of our money in silver. We left the office and walked in silence down the street. Suddenly Bobby turns to me and asks, "What does Jay mean by silver, Shel? If it's *bags of silver*, they'll be so heavy we won't be able to carry them into our apartments." We couldn't figure this out, so we ran back to the office and Jay explained very carefully exactly what he'd meant by investing in silver.' Once it had been explained, they both understood and De Niro promptly put it out of his mind, to get back to his real business of creating characters, with his close friend Scorsese.

By this time the pair had worked out their own technique of verbal shorthand when working on the set, able to communicate intricate thoughts through a series of quick shrugs, gestures and quiet whispers. When asked what exactly happened between them, Scorsese replied, 'The real stuff between me and Bob is private.' He later expanded a bit: 'Bob and I trust one another; we're friends. We get excited about the same things, distracted

by the same things, like when people make too much noise on
the set! We take names. They're not allowed back .... Bob and I
have this thing, that a movie set is like a church. No
nonbelievers allowed.'

After his separation from his family, this kind of complete
trust was what De Niro most needed, for in *Raging Bull* he
would strip away every layer of himself and build his Jake La
Motta from the bones up. It was a character who'd tax every
fibre of his talent, body and concentration and was not an easy
one for either the star to tell or the director to orchestrate. Their
shared sense of purpose served them well.

One of Martin Scorsese's first decisions was to shoot the film
in black-and-white; that was the vision he had, and he
demanded that it be realized that way on the screen. When his
mind first began twirling around the brutal saga of Jake La
Motta, it was very clear to him that it was a black-and-white
story – there was little grey in La Motta's life. *Rocky* and its
follow-ups had been created for Technicolor, but Scorsese saw
the life of 'the Bronx Bull' in the texture of its time-frame: the
chiaroscuro of the forties and fifties newsreels and early
television shows which had been the principal channellers and
chroniclers of La Motta's career.

Today, in the midst of the colourization wars where classic
films of the past are being coloured by computers,* it's a wonder
Scorsese obtained financing for the film at all (and, ironically,
from the same men who produced *Rocky*). He later admitted as
much, but for *Raging Bull* his vision was right on target, and it
shortly made *Rocky* look like an over-coloured and over-muscled
cartoon. In *Rocky*'s fight scenes blood flows as if from a leaky
ketchup bottle, while in *Raging Bull* it explodes from the boxer's
faces in long, horrifying spurts as the mind of the viewer does
the colouring.

Raging Bull was a project that had been on De Niro's mind for
quite a while. He'd first read a copy of La Motta's book way
back, when he was filming *The Godfather Part II* in Sicily, and had

---

* Flagrant examples of the most controversial colourizations include *Dark
Victory* with Bette Davis, Jimmy Stewart's *It's a Wonderful Life*, and *Casablanca*, the
most favourite of Bogart's films. For seldom-seen films, such as Clark Gable and
Hedy Lamarr's *Boom Town*, colourization has meant a new lease of life, since so
many black-and-white films are no longer shown on television at all due to their
early over-exposure. Purists howl, though, that *Citizen Kane* will soon be
bastardized by the colourizers.

then sent it on to Scorsese. He knew immediately it was movie
material on a grand scale. Also he was quick to acknowledge his
childhood fantasies about the macho fighters who'd peopled his
early youth, be they legitimate boxers with a faded pair of
Golden Gloves in the closet or just the rambunctious closet
fighter who does his best sparring in a bar after a long night of
juke-box music and beer. 'Something at the center of it was very
good for me,' he said. Also he was of an age to remember La
Motta's glory days.

'I was interested in fighters. The way they walk, the weight
thing – they always blow up – and there was just something
about Jake La Motta that was, for me, interesting. I wanted to
play a fighter – just like a child wants to be somebody else.'

Much has already been written about De Niro's remarkable
transformation into the former boxing star, from muscled youth
to obese middle-age, yet the underlying sense of dedication it
took to do it cannot be understated. It was a gruelling,
mind-numbing example of Method acting at its highest level,
and he had La Motta to thank in large part.

When the film idea became a reality, Jake was still coasting on
the book success of his story but was immediately interested in
helping out on the film version. Scorsese signed him on as
consultant, and his first job was teaching Little Italy's De Niro
an authentic Bronx accent. His second was to teach him how to
box. He worked for months before filming began with Bobby in
the boxing ring, helping the star to imitate his famous old
crouching style and general demeanour. La Motta had been
nothing less than an exhibitionist during his champion years,
and these details, down to his entrance into a ring swathed in a
hooded tiger-striped robe, were essential to his image.

The pair trained daily at New York's Gramercy Gym, and Jake
has said, 'I guess in the first six months we boxed a thousand
rounds, a half-hour straight every day. ... [Bobby] wouldn't
train unless he wore headgear and mouthpieces because he
knew he was starting to get through my defenses.' De Niro
turned himself into a finely tuned boxing-machine, so much so
that, according to La Motta, the former champ eventually
suffered '...from black eyes and my upper teeth caps were
busted, cost United Artists $4,000 to get them redone.' By the
time this sparring was finished, he said in awesomely honest
tones, 'I guess I'd rank Bobby in the first top twenty

middleweights, I swear.' He'd boasted at the beginning that, 'By the time I've finished teaching De Niro how to fight like me, he'll be able to box professionally.' For once in his life La Motta was totally correct.

During these punishing months, Bobby added pounds of muscle to his basically slender frame, and when the film actually started, he didn't stop, sparring regularly in a ring that had been specially built for him on the studio backlot so that he could keep his raging spirit up between takes. During this he told a reporter, 'I gained about twenty pounds for Jake and I'm still puttin' it on. I see so many fight movies where the actors are out of shape, I don't believe them. So I come to the gym here – they rigged up a special one – and work out every day … I've [even] got Sylvester Stallone's trainer.'

De Niro was learning more than just a Bronx accent and boxing basics from his teacher – he was also getting a lesson in celebrity survival. 'The world is full of guys who can't wait to come up to you in a bar to show you how tough they are,' he said. 'What Jake taught me was how to take punishment. But I'm not anxious to demonstrate the point.'

The ultimate test of La Motta's tutelage came when Bobby actually climbed into a Brooklyn boxing ring and fought three real fights. Billed as 'the Young La Motta', he won two of the three and heartily justified Jake's boast of his newly developed prowess.

Scorsese and De Niro worked together to structure the film in such a way that Bobby could literally grow into his part. The fight scenes covering La Motta's controversial career and headlined bouts with, among others, Suger Ray Robinson and Marcel Cerdan, from whom he won the middleweight title, actually comprised only fifteen minutes of the finished film but were necessary to shoot all at once at the beginning of production, when his body and boxing ability were at their peak. Once they had been shot, Bobby could devote himself to the disintegration of La Motta, a long period which required more personal research than the bang and slam of the canvas ring.

His research into Jake's life took him to Florida, where he spent time with La Motta's ex-wife, Vickie, and their daughter Stephanie, who were both willing to add their personal insight. Still a stunning blonde of close to fifty (she'd married La Motta

while still a teenager), Vickie was making the most of this
new-found celebrity; she would shortly pose for *Playboy*
magazine as well as produce and star in an exercise video for
middle-aged women. Digging into the memorabilia of her
turbulent life with Jake, she showed De Niro home movies of
the couple and their three children which had been taken over
the early years of her marriage. Scorsese later used the idea of
home movies for *Raging Bull's* only colour sequences,
interspersing the brightly hued snippets of his family life with
graphically violent fight scenes of his rise to the top.

Vickie was immediately taken with Bobby, telling *Playboy* in a
1981 interview that he reminded her so much of the young Jake
that she wanted to go to bed with him: 'I wanted to. In fact, I
thought: How could I not? An affair seemed the most normal
thing to do. But Bob wanted things to be businesslike. I should
have just attacked him or something. But I got shy. If I were just
attracted to him sexually and didn't like him, I would have
known just how to make it happen. But I was intimidated and
did everything wrong.'

Her twenty-eight-year-old daughter faced a more difficult
problem with De Niro, as just being near him brought back
many conflicting memories. She'd told him the good and the
bad of her father but was still surprised at the portrait of him
that finally emerged on screen. 'It was kinda scary,' she told a
London magazine. 'You know, I'd been really friendly with
Robert. We'd gone through my father's life and I'd told him
about the side that people didn't know about. He was really a
loving father … He's actually a guy who cares for his family.'

Another reason for Stephanie's dissatisfaction with the movie
might well rest on the fact that she wasn't in it. During their
sessions together they had talked about the possibility of her
playing her own mother in the film, but, 'Robert couldn't handle
that. He couldn't cope with being married in the film to
someone he thought of as his daughter.' All she ended up with
was a bit part and a chip on her shoulder.

At the time when Stephanie might well have thought she was
really in the running for the part, any chance of it was dispelled
when Scorsese met a young Bronx blonde named Cathy
Moriarty.

A complete unknown, her photograph had been spotted by
actor Joe Pesci who was to play Jake's manager/brother, Joey, in

the film. He was at a nightclub in Mount Vernon, New York, one evening and happened to look at the shot of a local beauty-contest winner and realized, 'She's a dead-ringer for Vickie La Motta.' He quickly introduced her to Scorsese and De Niro, and they were instantly intrigued. She'd turned eighteen the day she met them and was happy to admit it – 'For once I didn't have to lie about my age.' The sharp-eyed beauty was the third child of a close-knit Irish family and had been on her own for a while, '…working at different jobs – I was working in the garment district at that time – but every time I got a job, I became a different person. I just put on different voices, made up stories, playing a game with myself. So you see, acting wasn't something new for me.'

The movie's casting director, Cis Corman, told *American Film* magazine that, 'As soon as she walked into my office I knew we had our Vickie. Cathy possessed a sophistication that many young women in the forties had. She was older than her years.'

De Niro and Scorsese recognized it too but took their time making sure of it. 'For three months I would go down to the city to read for them,' the Bronx-born newcomer said. 'It was like taking private acting lessons. They never once said that I had the part or anything, and I knew they were seeing other actresses, too. I was just happy to be learning about acting from two of the best people in the business …'

She quickly learned from De Niro's intensity how to become Vickie and how to stay in character. 'It was easy, because he was Jake all the time, and then I'd be Vickie. Since he felt it so much, I was able to feel it too.'

Cathy Moriarty fitted the part like a glove, with her naturally deep voice and Bronx accent. Also she could relate to Vickie's precociousness – Vickie had entered La Motta's life when she was only fifteen: 'When I was fifteen, I wasn't fifteen, if you know what I mean. I was a little wild … I was adventurous.'

But learn about acting she did, even if it was occasionally the hard way. She revealed more to *American Film*: 'Marty never told me directly what to do, especially in the fight scenes. He just told me what was going to happen, and they filled in my reactions.' In one scene the jealous La Motta thinks she's been flirting, and Scorsese and De Niro told her they'd fake his violent reaction. Instead, with the cameras rolling, De Niro really slapped her. 'I didn't know what to do, I was so shocked.

But that was the way Vickie would have reacted.'

She later added, 'I used to hate them because they didn't tell me things. Bobby got to meet Jake, Joe [Pesci] got to meet Joey, but they wouldn't even let me talk to Vickie. Now I'm glad they didn't. They didn't want me to react to certain stories she would tell me; they wanted me to react to what *they* had to say about Jake and Vickie ... Sometimes I did feel intimidated, but I think that's the way they wanted me to feel.'

The actress sensed parallels between herself and Vickie. As Vickie had married La Motta at fifteen, Cathy had been dating older men at the same age, and her street-learned sensibilities held her in good stead. 'There were times that I wanted to cry, but I decided that I didn't want to, that it was important not to show I had been hurt. And you know, I talked with Vickie after we finished [the film] and asked her if she ever cried. And she said, "Not while Jake was around. I always waited until he was gone."'

As the movie went ahead, Cathy Moriarty's earthy manner became increasingly necessary as her film husband changed before her eyes. After completion of the scenes where Jake and Vickie meet and marry and he fights his earliest bouts and wins the championship, production was halted so that Bobby could make himself over into the grossly overweight La Motta of his later years. Gradually the beautifully muscled body built up over long months of intense training and exercise began to disappear under layers of flab. 'It was Bobby's idea,' Scorsese told *American Film*, 'and when he told me about it, I thought it was great.'

With the picture shut down, De Niro decided to return to Italy and revisit some of the places he'd come to know and care for while making *1900*. It was the beginning of a four-month-long eating binge during which he'd bloat his body up from its normal 155 pounds to almost 215. The reason for this was dedication to the part, pure and simple, but when the public saw the results, they became obsessed with what he'd done to himself, and it became one of the most consistently irritating queries he'd face in the months ahead.

But it was fun at the beginning. 'At first I thought "Gee, well I can just pig out",' which is exactly what he did, adding, 'It was very easy. I just had to get up at six-thirty in the morning and eat breakfast at seven in order to digest my food to eat lunch at twelve or one in order to digest my food to eat a nice dinner at seven at night. So it was three square meals a day, that's all. You know, pancakes, beer, milk,' and lots of pasta as well.

Facing it pragmatically, he said, 'I used to carry my son a lot on my shoulders, and I'd think – this is what I have to gain, this much weight. By the time I had gained fifty pounds it was hard to tie my shoe, I couldn't bend, my thighs were rubbing against each other, I was getting rashes and my heels were starting to hurt.'

During the long summer of 1979 he virtually ate his way across Europe. 'I went to France and went to all the two-star and three-star restaurants and stuffed myself. I kept using those French Alka-Seltzer – but in a week I gained seven pounds.'

By then, however, the fun was over. 'I was very uncomfortable with the weight. But we gave ourselves a deadline when we were going to shoot [again], whatever the weight was.' And when that deadline came, the cameras rolled and yet another 'new' De Niro lumbered in front of them, his nose thickened by make-up experts and his body unrecognizably thickened by the great chefs of Europe. Said Scorsese, 'Bobby would get tired pretty easily from carrying all that weight.'

Bobby later told *Life* magazine that, 'A doctor was monitoring my health, and he wasn't too happy about it. I had a little problem with my blood pressure ... I was huffing and puffing, and my breathing sounded strange ... My daughter got so she was terribly embarrassed for her friends to see me. After all I looked like an animal.' Considering that he had to act like one for the rest of the film, he was in perfect shape for it.

La Motta's life after losing the middleweight crown was one long and bumpy slide into headlined obscurity. A contradiction in terms? Not in Jake's case, for the worse his life got, the more the newspapers chronicled it. After his retirement from the ring in 1956, he opened a nightclub in Miami where he appeared as MC, offering a weak comedy routine to the patrons who thrived on his second-rate celebrity. One night his massive ego trips him up and he's later arrested for having allowed teenage girls to drink and make friends in his club. (In real life Jake was accused of being an out-and-out pimp.) Gaoled, he's thrown into solitary confinement in a scene where one can feel the enormous energy of the wasted life of the Raging Bull as De Niro howls into the darkness of his tiny cell and slams his hands into the wall as he'd used to pummel a punch-bag. La Motta had fought and scrambled his whole life to become a champion, bucking the Mob and alienating his brother in the process, only to lose it all in a shameful arrest and six months on a Florida chain gang.

Before the success of his autobiography, La Motta had been working as a bouncer/comic at a New York City strip club. The climb back to respectability was a mentally torturous one – and only an actor like De Niro could have made the sordid mess believable and sympathetic.

One scene in particular illustrates both La Motta's personality and De Niro's interpretation of it. He's working in a club with a sign outside announcing his programme of interpreting various pieces from the works of Shakespeare, Tennessee Williams and Paddy Chayevsky. De Niro/La Motta plays the scene from Chayevsky's *On the Waterfront*, the 'I coulda been a contender' speech made famous by Marlon Brando, and does an astonishing job. He's literally doing La Motta doing Brando from the movie, and the words ring with an authenticity that even Brando had not given them.

In an uneasy, easily unlikeable film, because of its blatant depiction of the brutality of the boxing world and the men who people it, De Niro is the glue that cements that world into an understandable, if unlikeable, whole. 'To call *Raging Bull* a boxing picture is ridiculous,' Scorsese later said. 'It's sports but it's [also] something to do with living. Jake La Motta takes on aspects of everybody.'

Once it was over, De Niro experienced a feeling of depression, partly from trying to lose the weight he'd put on and also from realizing he'd done what might be a once-in-a-lifetime acting job. (Ironically weight had always played a large part in La Motta's life as well – only he was always trying to keep it off to stay in the middleweight range.)

Bobby's depression lifted when the film opened to the astonishment of audiences and critics. They couldn't believe what they were seeing, and he was quickly besieged with commendation for his uncompromising work. *Raging Bull* was nominated for a total of eight Academy Awards – for De Niro, Joe Pesci, Cathy Moriarty and director Scorsese, plus Best Picture, Cinematography, Sound and Film Editing. It proved that Scorsese was indisputably a director capable of creating a classic, perhaps his own *Citizen Kane*, with this story of a man's rise and then his pathetic slide downhill. Reviewers compared it with *Rocky* – 'a say-nothing stew of weepy pulp compared to the battering bestiality of a *Raging Bull*' – with one adding that he hoped Scorsese '…would end his Italian-American guilt trip and stop exposing mean-tempered, self-destructive characters like La Motta'. Any controversy only convinced the director that his original vision of the film was true; it was received in a black-and-white manner, with people either loving it or hating it, with no middle ground.

The Hollywood Establishment reacted in much the same way, at once eager to recognize Scorsese and company's brilliance with all those Academy nominations but unwilling to give it landslide approval. The film grossed over $10 million, which made it neither hit nor a flop with the let's-go-to-the-movies-for-a-good-time crowd yet strong enough for the producers to know that their message had reached a large number of people. It could have been that the romance of *Rocky* and the cock-eyed glamour of Sylvester Stallone kept people away from the realism of *Raging Bull*, but the millions who did see it were rewarded with the blatant facts of life of the boxing world, and that type of reality was to serve as a cornerstone of the new decade.

At least the Academy was ready to acknowledge this when De Niro won its Best Actor Award, besting Robert Duvall's *The Great Santini*, John Hurt's *Elephant Man*, Jack Lemmon's *Tribute* and Peter O'Toole's performance in *The Stuntman*. Of all these extremely personalized portrayals of man in crisis, Bobby emerged the winner. He was extolled as being the embodiment of the Method, living his part so intensely that Hal Hinson of *Sight and Sound* said, 'The identification is so complete that the distinction between actor and role becomes blurred – he enters a character the way that a somnambulist enters a trance.'

For his part, the real La Motta was ecstatic, saying, 'Bobby came from heaven. He gave me a whole new lease of life.' The film gave him another period of celebrity in which to bask, even though he privately thought the film made him more of a monster than he'd really been. Said Vickie, 'He sees there's beauty in it, and he sees there's honesty but he still gets hurt.'

As for Cathy Moriarty, the film seemed to be the beginning of a major career. Though she lost the Oscar to Mary Steenburgen's *Melvin and Howard*, she was quickly signed to co-star with De Niro's friend John Belushi and Dan Ackroyd in *Neighbors*. That turned out to be the kind of flop that could kill the most promising of careers, but fate had an even harsher hand to deal Cathy, when, in 1982, she and her husband were in a terrible car crash that completely halted her career for several years. The 'Bronx Madonna' of *Raging Bull* wasn't able to work again until 1985, when she was set to star with Jack Nicholson in *Two Jakes*, the much-touted sequel to *Chinatown*. When that production was cancelled just before shooting was to begin, she didn't work again until 1988's *White of the Eye*. She said that her role in it '…offers a wide range of emotions to play – fear, anger, love. That's rare and it's sad.' And how much it must have reminded her of the life of Vickie La Motta which had brought her so vividly to fame!

For De Niro the critical success of *Raging Bull* and the accompanying Oscar brought on a period of quiet, acting-wise at least. It would be well over a year before he'd appear on screen again – but it wouldn't be a dull year.

10   *Collaring De Niro*

Robert De Niro has never been a man to savour success for the sake of it. When *Raging Bull* and its many accolades descended on him, it was only natural for him to want to share these rewards with his family. He was crazy about his adopted daughter and four-year-old son, and he saw them often, both on his own and with Diahnne, but a reconciliation with his wife didn't happen. Their relationship seemed to have settled into parallel grooves, and both seemed content with it. He, as always, was mulling over what next to do professionally while dieting and getting back into good physical shape, while she quietly pursued her own acting aspirations, though more on a talk than an action level.

Once Bobby had dieted off his Jake La Motta bulk and worked through the mild depression it had brought on, he travelled back to Italy, but this time his reception would not be one of open-armed welcome.

The actor mind of De Niro has always been a quiet and watchful one and, if anything after his winning a second Oscar, his well-developed need for privacy was greater than ever. When he landed at Rome Airport later that spring, he was even more understated than ever. So much so that he made international headlines when airport security men mistook the reticent star for a terrorist! Shots of him with his arms up and backed against a wall while a soldier patted him down for concealed weapons made newspaper front pages around the world. It proved to be an extremely embarrassing moment, not made any easier by De Niro's inability to identify himself. (You can't help wondering if the idea for some movie story wasn't clicking through his head at the time!) For ninety minutes he was held under lock and key by airport police before his identity could be verified and he was finally released.

As an actor he also faced questions like, what to do as a follow-up to *Raging Bull*? Looking for a complete change of pace, he couldn't have found a more astounding one than when he picked *True Confessions* – as in it he would be playing a powerful Catholic clergyman in the Los Angeles of 1948, just about as far away from the boxing world and the Bronx as one could get.

His role as Monsignor Desmond Spellacy took him into a realm of religious conflict as opposed to the physical, and he approached it with a sense of quiet dignity he'd never shown on screen before, with the possible exception of *1900*. Suddenly the sodden clown of an ex-boxing champ was transformed into a steely voiced prelate who is both coolly ambitious and spiritually tormented. From his first moment on screen, De Niro assumes a businesslike piety as he goes about running the affairs of the archdiocese. He exudes a crisp finality in his job – look at the golf-course scene when, after calmly announcing he's cutting off business relations with a crooked construction boss, he taps his ball straight and clear into the hole.

This was a facet of De Niro's talent new to the mainstream. In so many films, from *Mean Streets* to *Taxi Driver* to *Raging Bull*, he'd played the alien from the system, the social outsider scrambling for an identity, but *True Confessions* saw him become the epitome of the company man.

The part called for a juggling act of emotions, not to mention a clear ecclesiastical knowledge which he immediately set out to attain.

When an actor meets his match on screen, it's always a joy to sit back and watch the sparks fly, which is what happened when Robert Duvall was signed to play the monsignor's policeman brother, Tom. Though both had appeared in *The Godfather Part II*, they'd had no scenes together because of the different time-frames of the story, but Duvall was Bobby's kind of actor, dedicated, explorative and thoroughly professional. Ironically, just the year before, they had been up against each other for the Oscar that Bobby had won over Duvall's terrific performance in *The Great Santini*, and they'd been looking forward to the time they'd work together.

As the Spellacy brothers whose uneasy truce is ripped apart by their contrasting worlds and morals, the two stars had a field day, easily jumping back in time to Los Angeles after World War II and into the skins of the ambitious Irishmen who each took a

classic route to respectability – Tom to the police academy and
Des to the seminary.

De Niro, as it turned out, practically joined a seminary for his
role as the priest who rises to monsignor and almost
singlehandedly brings his diocese out of the red and into the
black as he cuts a few of his spiritual corners in the bargain.
Months before the cameras rolled, he began his religious trip
back in time, studying and practising the Catholic Mass in Latin
as it was performed in the forties. As the picture opens, he's
seen officiating at the altar, and every phrase and move is
flawlessly realistic.

With the assistance of the film's religious technical adviser,
Father Henry Fehren, De Niro had assiduously studied Church
dogma and procedure, even to the point of wearing authentic
vestments during film rehearsals. Not only was the film's
director, Ulu Grosbard, impressed – 'By the time he was ready
to film, he talked like a priest. He *was* a priest' – but so was
Father Fehren, who noted how De Niro wanted to understand
not only the Church routine but also 'the sense, feeling and
tradition of what the Church was in 1948'. Bing Crosby had won
an Academy Award playing a priest *circa* 1945, but his
happy-go-lucky prelate was nothing compared with De Niro's
re-creation of the real thing. Father Fehren said quietly, 'He may
be the most authentic priest ever seen on the screen.'

This homework was vital to De Niro, because the priest had to
look and act totally committed, thus helping to hide the
shallowness of his vocation. At one point his monsignor admits
that his love of the Church has always been less than his love of
succeeding, but it was the best way for him to escape the Irish
slums, just as police work was for his brother.

The plot of *True Confessions* is hung around the murder of a
Hollywood 'party girl' – read 'whore' – who's murdered in the
same grisly way as the real-life Black Dahlia was in the late
forties: her body is found cut in two and drained of blood.
Brother Tom is the chief detective on the scene and as he works
on the case uncovers clues which lead by a circuitous route back
to business ties of the archdiocese and thus to his brother. A
construction tsar who's built many schools and churches for the
archdiocese, with Desmond's co-operation, is at the bottom of
the mystery. The exposure of this man played in grandiose style

by Charles Durning, will bring scandal to Desmond's reputation and negate any chances of his rising higher in the Church order, dissolving them in the heat of unsavoury headlines. Tom confronts his brother in the confessional and tells him this must be done. Des, now cognizant of the many ramifications of his power, both the good and the bad, wearily says he no longer cares and that his brother must do what he thinks is right. Tom presents his evidence, his brother falls from grace, and the pair are only finally reunited years later when Des is dying and summons his brother to the tiny desert parish where he's long been exiled. They talk over their grievances and forgive each other, and the film ends with their looking at the fenced-in patch of sand that will eventually be their burial place.

To say the plot is convoluted is an understatement but, when watching it, the viewer is so taken up with the wealth of performances that it almost works. The director was sufficiently comfortable with his actors to let them indulge themselves, and at a wedding reception of the construction boss's daughter we see Durning do an Irish jig very reminiscent of what he'd later do in *The Best Little Whorehouse in Texas*, for which he received an Oscar nomination. Excellent too was Kenneth McMillan as Tom's right-hand man in the police department. Other seasoned pros included Ed Flanders, Cyril Cusack, Burgess Meredith and Rose Gregorio.

For once De Niro didn't have to go to physical extremes for his part. In fact, he was still slowly shedding his *Raging Bull* poundage, which only served to give his character a prosperous look. This was obviously a man who knew a good wine when offered one and who didn't skimp when ordering a meal. His appearance served to emphasize his shaky religious base and the practicality of his business life.

Duvall received top honours from reviewers for his crusty detective, a man who's spent his life looking at its seamier sides. *The New York Times* said succinctly that, 'No American film in a long time has presented such a conjunction of acting talents.' Critics enjoyed all the facets of *True Confessions*, including its authentic look – it was shot in Los Angeles at some sixty locations – but the over-all effort seemed hardly worth the trouble. De Niro and Duvall tied for the Best Actor award at the Venice Film Festival, but at home the film was virtually ignored, except for the curiosity that always surrounds an Oscar-winner's follow-up picture. The old phrase 'No one sets out to make a bad movie' certainly applied in this case. All the money and effort were there on screen but what few theatregoers there were were left with the feeling that it had been much ado about not very much!

One reason for public apathy at this time might have stemmed from the fact that so many stars were making headlines with their personal lives, particularly the tragic ones.

The early years of the eighties were marked by a series of shocking celebrity deaths: Natalie Wood drowned off Catalina Island under mysterious circumstances: Grace Kelly, the former Hollywood queen who became Monaco's Serene Highness, hurtled off a French mountainside after suffering a stroke at the wheel of her car; and on 5 March 1982 comedian John Belushi overdosed on drugs in a bungalow of a swanky Hollywood hotel. Of them all, Belushi's death was perhaps the most sensational, since several star names cropped up in its investigation, the most surprising of which was De Niro's.

The star has always been obsessively quiet about his private life, and Belushi's death brought an unwelcome light onto it which resulted in headlines and speculation. Actors who become suddenly famous about the same time often gravitate towards each other, as if to confirm their own celebrity in a private club of friendship. Just after De Niro won his *Godfather* Oscar in 1974, Belushi exploded on the scene via television's *Saturday Night Live*, and the pair became friends in a loosely constructed group that included Robin Williams and Carrie Fisher.

When De Niro was based in Hollywood, as he was during production of *True Confessions*, it was natural that he'd spend time at the most popular hangout, which at that time was a club called 'On the Rox' on Sunset Strip. Located over the Roxy nightclub, it was more like a large and comfortable living-room than the private club it was, and celebrities could relax there away from the spotlight and the crazy fans to enjoy the company of their peers in undisturbed surroundings.

There was always shop talk, though, especially in Belushi's case, as his enormous transitional success from television to films via *Animal House* seemed to be in jeopardy after a couple of

failed films, such as Steven Spielberg's gigantic bomb *1941*.*
Belushi was frankly in awe of De Niro, calling him 'Bobby D',
and talked acting with him at every opportunity. The pair
became even friendlier when De Niro stayed at the Château
Marmont Hotel when in town; Bobby in a penthouse, Belushi in
a private bungalow.

In Bob Woodward's book *Wired: The Short Life & Fast Times of
John Belushi*, he asserts that the pair used cocaine together on
occasions, which in itself isn't really remarkable, since everyone
else in town at that time was doing it too. It was not then
perceived to be the dangerous killer it's labelled today, and De
Niro, as his past shows, seemed always willing to experience a
new sensation if it might give him further insight into either a
character or himself. De Niro had a built-in alarm system,
however, that kept him from going over the edge, and he was
quick to realize when other people were headed that way – as
Belushi was in early march 1982.

Unhappy at the failure of his recent movies – he'd hated what
he'd seen of *Neighbors*, which co-starred Cathy Moriarty – and
his lack of success at launching a new project called *Noble Rot*,
Belushi was disenchanted with Hollywood as a place and the
people who made its creative decisions. On the night he died he
was at 'On the Rox', railing against the people he felt were
trying to stifle his creativity. One of his last printable lines to
friends there was, reportedly, 'Thank God this will be my last
night in L.A.' The following day he was scheduled to return to
New York City.

De Niro was at the club that night too and made a loose
arrangement to meet Belushi later at his hotel bungalow.
(Afterwards De Niro's people put out the word that one major
topic the pair had to discuss was Belushi's possible participation
in *Once Upon a Time in America*, a film De Niro was considering at
the time.) According to *Wired*, De Niro did show up at Belushi's
place, appearing at the sliding glass doors at the rear and staying
only a few minutes. (Each bungalow is self-contained with a
private back yard where super-shy celebrities can catch some
sun without going to the main swimming-pool.)

---

* Belushi's mildly successful *Continental Divide* with Blair Brown had once
almost been a De Niro vehicle which would have reteamed him with Jill
Clayburgh, but Belushi inherited the part much later down the line and did one
of his best acting jobs as the sportswriter who falls for an independent outdoor
girl.

The next morning all hell broke loose at the Marmont when Belushi was found dead of a drug overdose. Almost as soon as she found out, the hotel's manager took a phone call from De Niro's penthouse. He'd been trying to reach John for some time but had been unable to get through. She had to tell him, as diplomatically as possible, that the situation was bad. De Niro became instantly alerted by the tone of her voice and asked if John was sick. When she replied, 'It's really bad,' Bobby got the message and understood that his friend was gone. He broke down, sobbing over the phone.

As Belushi had idolized De Niro, so had he appreciated the comedian's rare talent, but the Crown Prince of the Method School of acting had no way of knowing that the Clown Prince of the Movies was so deeply addicted to cocaine – Belushi called it 'Hitler's drug' because of the sense of power it gave him. He was devastated by the comic's death and totally withdrew into his penthouse for several long days, watching Belushi performances from *Saturday Night Live* over and over again on his video recorder, while downstairs television and newspaper reporters prowled the premises in the wake of the sensational death. And the fact that De Niro had spent time with Belushi the night he died led to unsavoury publicity. One of the few friends he allowed into his suite said he acted 'scary but very controlled'.

Newspapers headlined 'Actors To Face Quiz Over Scandal Of Comic's Death' after De Niro and Robin Williams had been named by Belushi's girlfriend, Cathy Smith, as being among the last to see him alive. She identified the stars in a tabloid article for which she was paid $10,000 – obviously not realizing that the only person she was really implicating was herself, as she also admitted to having supplied Belushi with the drugs that killed him and helping him inject them. Eventually De Niro gave a statement by phone to the grand jury investigating the case and then tried to put it out of his mind. The whole episode was so distastefully tragic to him that he's never publicly said a word about it, and likely never will. Any time a brave reporter brings up the subject, he's quickly cut off.

Any residual memory of the trauma of Belushi's sad dependence and death was undoubtedly put to some positive use in De Niro's next film, *The King of Comedy*. It marked his fifth movie with Martin Scorsese directing, and though the project had been milling in Scorsese's mind for years before that night at the Château Marmont in Hollywood, there were aspects of it that undeniably had been triggered by it.

The King of Comedy was basically about obsessive fans of the famous, and the chances they were willing to take to gain even a few minutes of a star's reflected glory. It typified many of the people Belushi surrounded himself with just before his death, although, in his case, it was would-be actresses and ageing groupies with drug connections to ease their way inside who were his downfall. De Niro and Scorsese would take this premise in another direction, but the message was the same: these people would do anything for that intimate glimpse of fame. In *The King of Comedy* that would mean literally taking them hostage and holding them to ransom for a slice of it.

While De Niro's life may have helped set the stage for this film, another part of it brought him face to face with himself when, at the end of September, headlines spelled out another story: *'Raging Bull* Baby Shocks Wife.'

The mother of this child was black singer Helena Springs, and the baby girl, whom he would eventually adopt, was named Nina Nadeja De Niro. When he discovered he was to be a father again, the actor reportedly deluged Helena with gifts, which included a new wardrobe and a sports car – but there was no talk of marriage. There wasn't any talk about a divorce from Diahnne either. Instead, she was surprisingly at work with him as his romantic interest in the new movie. The master juggler of acting seemed to be equally adept at handling the diverse parts of his private life.

11   *King for a Day*

The situation between De Niro and his estranged wife, Diahnne, actually served to help their work together in *The King of Comedy*, since he played a man who's been out of her sight, and mind, for quite a while. In their first scene together, Rupert Pupkin, an erstwhile comedian and former high school friend, comes into the rundown bar where Rita (Diahnne) works, sidles up to her and asks, 'How you been?' Rita stares blankly back at him and counters: 'Do I know you?'

This was the essence of their screen relationship, he the man who moves in and out of her life with disarming regularity while she tries in vain to cool his occasional ardour. Hoping to impress Rita, he shows her his autograph book. One signature she can't read but Rupert quickly points out, 'The more scribbled the name, the bigger the fame.' Their friends must have been only mildly surprised when Diahnne was cast in the role, because she was perfect for the part.

The King of Comedy wasn't meant to be a funny movie – and in that respect the talents of De Niro and Scorsese were not wasted. The ad campaign for the picture featured a widely smiling, open-armed De Niro wearing a terrible polka-dotted jacket, poised before a cheering audience proclaiming him the 'new' King of Comedy, but the audience quickly finds out that the pose is only the fantasy of poor Rupert Pupkin. Fantasy or not, though, they are also fast to realize that it's one he's totally prepared to live out at any cost.

By this, their fifth film together, the director/star pair of Scorsese and De Niro was a well-oiled machine, totally synchronized and having already proven theirs to be one of the most creative partnerships in movie history. And, once again, they'd be tackling such an uncomfortable subject that all their respective skills would be needed in pulling it off.

The idea for *The King of Comedy* first came to screenwriter Paul Zimmerman back in 1974 when he saw a David Susskind television show about the most 'fringe' element of show business, the autograph hounds, those sadly possessed people who line up nightly outside theatre exits and studio gates in order to snare a celebrity's signature, an insatiable bunch who stalk their prey with organized precision. Zimmerman '...realized that autograph hounds are just like assassins except that one carries a pen instead of a gun'. The idea of them fascinated him, and he went several steps further by writing a screenplay about one who tries to make his star fantasies a reality – and bizarrely succeeds.

Zimmerman's Rupert Pupkin is a man with a great deal of misplaced self-confidence. He wants desperately to escape his pathetic life in a basement surrounded by cardboard cutouts of his favourite stars and to join the ranks of the celebrated whose signatures he's been collecting all his life. Rupert wants to be a comedian – and after numerous auditions in front of his cardboard friends decides he's good enough to start at the top, on television's *Jerry Langford Show*. His unique way of getting there is what makes the movie into the exceedingly dark comedy it is.

After saving Langford, played to perfection by Jerry Lewis, from a mob of autograph-hunters,[*] Rupert tries to strike up an acquaintance with the star to get him to consider his material for the show. Langford does the 'drop by my office' routine, trying to get rid of him, but Rupert thinks he means it and that he'll shortly feature on Langford's show with the likes of Liza Minelli, Dr Joyce Brothers and Tony Randall. When Langford's secretary gives him back his tape and says he needs more 'experience', he's instantly sure that this brush-off is a mistake, that Langford never heard his routines.

Seeking to impress his reluctant friend Rita, he takes her to Langford's weekend home and forces them in as weekend guests, and then the pair proceed to relax and entertain themselves until Langford's return. When he's confronted with

---

[*] If the mob scene at Jerry's studio looks realistic, that's because it was based in fact. De Niro had personally interviewed real-life autograph hunters on their techniques and experiences and made sure these touches – not to mention several real collectors – were incorporated into the frantic scene. He and Scorsese even went to one man's home 'to see my collection'.

these intruders, he's forced to be blunt with Rupert, telling him he has no talent, that he'd only been trying to be civil and now to get out of his life.

With the help of his deeply disturbed and star-crazy friend Masha, played with manic gusto by Sandra Bernhard,* Pupkin decides to kidnap Langford and hold him for ransom – that being fifteen minutes of airtime on his show!

Their desperate scheme takes them all on a rollercoaster ride of clashing egos which ends with Langford bound to a chair in the girl's townhouse reading Rupert's ungrammatical terms over the phone to his producer. The deal is set, and Rupert performs his fifteen-minute routine – part of which Langford witnesses. After tricking the sex-crazed Masha into untying him, he escapes her house and, while fleeing down the street, sees a store window full of television sets all tuned into his show – starring that 'new' King of Comedy, Rupert Pupkin. And surprisingly, polka-dot jacket and all, he's being funny!

After the show and with FBI agents beside him, Rupert goes to the bar where Rita works. Still determined to impress her, he barges in and switches the television set over to *The Jerry Langford Show* so she can witness his triumph. That in itself would have made an interesting ending for the film, but Scorsese went further and in doing so angered many critics. Instead of Rupert's simply being carted off to an anonymous gaol cell, he becomes suddenly famous as a result of his crazy actions. In prison his criminal behaviour continues to pay off when he writes his autobiography, which is published to acclaim and success. When he's released, he re-débuts on television to a wildly acceptive audience. Then the screen goes black. The story is over, and Rupert Pupkin is its hero.

The King of Comedy was very much a family affair. Scorsese surrounded himself with many old friends and co-workers in putting it together, from its film editor and casting director (both from *Raging Bull*) to writer friends such as Martin Mardik, who played a drunk in the bar watching Rupert's performance. Scorsese's mother, Catherine, played Rupert's off-screen mother, while his brother showed up as another bar patron.

One stranger to this group, yet the one who would walk away with renewed respect and the best reviews, was Jerry Lewis.

---

* De Niro reportedly wanted Meryl Streep for the part but she was too busy.

Writer Zimmerman had said of his script that it was 'a film about the desperate need to exist publicly', and this description was one Lewis could easily relate to. Long over-indulged for his post-Dean Martin comedies (especially in France, where he's been practically beatified as a comedic saint), Lewis came to the film with his own history of being a television king of comedy à la Jerry Langford, albeit without his character's success. *The Jerry Lewis Show* ran for thirteen episodes in 1963 – about twelve too many according to one critic, who said that by the end of the run he'd '...immersed himself in a bath of self-pity and paranoia'. Lewis' career had been one of extreme ups and downs, and his casting as Langford was perfect: when Langford tries to explain to Rupert that his audition tape was overlooked because of the stresses of his job and the dizzying duties of running a major television show, you can sense his total honesty and experience. Lewis could easily have improvised his lines from his own chequered career.

Initially Scorsese wanted to go right to the top and have Johnny Carson play the Langford role, but movie-shy Johnny declined, mainly because he thought that by doing the part he might easily trigger someone to act out the plot in real life and kidnap him! He also felt that, if he was going to make a film, he would not choose one where he'd literally be playing himself. 'But he was very helpful,' Scorsese said. 'During shooting we'd call him up and ask questions. Every time we called, he said the same things: "What's the matter? You lose Jerry?" '

To research his climactic comedy routine, De Niro spent hours haunting the New York comedy clubs where young and undiscovered talent worked out their material. He wanted to maintain his distance from the mainstream and was quick to turn down Lewis' initial gestures of friendship, insisting he had to remain in character. He told Lewis, 'I wanna blow your head off. How can we have dinner?'

For the scene in Langford's country house where he explodes with rage towards Rupert, De Niro pulled another ploy, openly baiting Lewis with a barrage of anti-Semitic remarks in order to get the necessarily furious reaction. Lewis was astonished. 'I forgot the cameras were there. At the end, Marty couldn't just say "cut". I was going for Bobby's throat!'

Eventually, though, even Lewis' rampant ego came to appreciate Bobby's technique and talent. About the process of doing a scene with him, he told *People*. 'Take one, Bobby's getting oriented. By ten, you're watching magic, and in fifteen, you're seeing genius.'

To another interviewer he admitted that working for Scorsese and with De Niro was a once-in-a-lifetime chance that, '...any actor would remember for the rest of his life. It had to be the same kind of feeling actors had the first time they worked with the likes of Marlon Brando, Rod Steiger, Paul Newman and so on. He is the ultimate professional .... Actors always dream of their credits being the best possible. Well, I believe that no actor will ever enlist a greater credit than being able to say he worked with Robert De Niro and Martin Scorsese. I'm just proud to have been the third party.'

He should also have been proud of the performance they got from him, as it's easily the best of his later career. After his string of smash comedies partnered with Dean Martin, Lewis went slowly but steadily downward in one unfunny movie after another until 1967's *Don't Raise the Bridge, Lower the Water* left his career high and dry. His acting in *The King of Comedy* was a revelation but, oddly, didn't lead to more work.

Ironically that was also the movie fate of Sandra Bernhard, whose Masha easily deserved a Best Supporting Actress nomination. 'From the moment I auditioned for the part, I was obsessed with getting it,' she said later, and it is a wonderful matching of actor to role. One can only speculate what the Ice Queen Meryl Streep would have done with that volcanic junkpile of loud-mouthed femininity.

The film cost over $20 million to produce but made only a fraction of that at theatres. Perhaps audiences were feeling much like its star and director, for whom the film brought back unhappy memories. They made the picture as a statement expressing their shared views of the dangers of celebrity, and that was something they'd both experienced the hard way.

When John Hinckley tried to assassinate President Reagan in March 1981, federal investigators were quick to reveal that he'd been inspired by De Niro's Travis Bickle in *Taxi Driver*, who, at one point, stalks a presidential candidate. They attested that Hinckley had watched the film some fifteen times, and three psychiatrists testified that he had eventually reached a point where he thought he *was* Bickle. The ensuing publicity surrounding this news made great fodder for the tabloids and

Robert De Niro, as baseball player Bruce Pearson, stares with longing at his conniving girlfriend Katie, played by Ann Wedgeworth in *Bang the Drum Slowly*.

Vito Corleone (De Niro) struggles with his family's enemies to settle a bloody Sicilian debt of honour in *The Godfather Part II*.

A 'family portrait' of the young Vito, now the new Godfather on New York's Lower East Side. Francesca De Sapio played De Niro's wife in *The Godfather Part II*.

A teenage prostitute played by a young Jodie Foster is befriended by Travis Bickle (De Niro) in *Taxi Driver*. Her youthful sexuality reportedly obsessed John Hinckley, the man who tried to assassinate President Reagan in 1981.

On the set of *Taxi Driver*, De Niro listens attentively to his director and friend, Martin Scorsese. Theirs has been one of the most controversial screen partnerships in movie history.

Two international acting legends, De Niro and France's Gerard Depardieu, during the making of the multi-million dollar epic *1900*. An instant and lasting friendship – and mutual professional respect – came from this screen pairing.

Monroe Stahr (De Niro) dances with the mysterious Kathleen Moore (Ingrid Boulting) in one of the few happy moments in *The Last Tycoon*.

Liza Minelli, as singer Angie Evans, looks on in delight as Jimmy Doyle (De Niro) backs her song with his saxophone in *New York, New York*. De Niro practised for hours a day to perfect his musical scenes.

Director Michael Cimino discusses a tense moment in the uneasy reunion of De Niro and Meryl Streep near the end of *The Deer Hunter*. The pair quickly became each other's favourite actor.

After completing a perilous helicopter jump in *The Deer Hunter*, De Niro pulls co-star Jon Savage from the raging waters of the River Kwai. They had insisted on doing the dangerous stunt themselves – and it almost cost them their lives.

Michael Cimino directs a riveted De Niro during the shooting of the brutal prisoner-of-war sequences in *The Deer Hunter*. The violent honesty of these scenes has since been widely imitated in subsequent films about the Vietnam War.

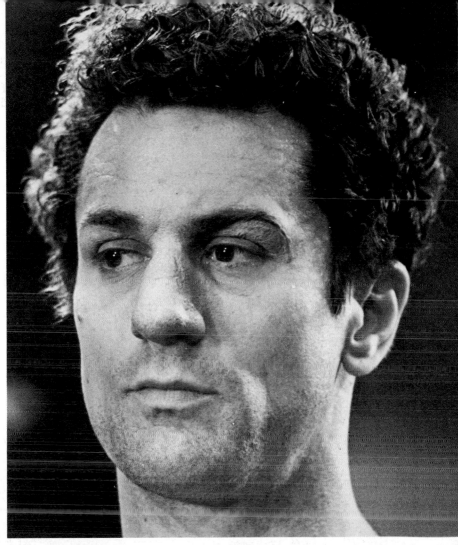

With curly hair and a nosepiece, De Niro makes an awesome young Jake La Motta in Martin Scorsese's masterpiece, *Raging Bull*.

Bloated with sixty extra pounds, De Niro imitates an older Jake La Motta at the microphone of his Miami nightclub.

also caused De Niro personal distress. For the first time in his career he'd been confronted by fans in the street demanding that he recite Bickle's infamous line: 'Ya talkin' to me?' 'Don't they realize I'm not that guy?' he'd ask Scorsese plaintively. Since then it has become another subject he refuses to talk about.

Scorsese was equally shocked over the controversy, telling Patricia Bosworth, 'I refused to comment for six months. I didn't feel like making another film for a while, and I'd never felt that way before.' He was also quick to add that he had no regrets about having made *Taxi Driver*. 'It was not an irresponsible act – it was a responsible one. Bob and I both thought so at the time. We both thought, this is something we're attracted to – let's go for it! Movies don't kill people. People kill people.'

If anything, it was the enormity of De Niro's talent and performances that helped make Travis *and* Rupert understandable to the thoughtful moviegoer. 'Part of Bob's great gift is his ability to play a character like Rupert Pupkin and bring out the sympathetic, even vulnerable qualities. The same was true of his portrayal of Travis in *Taxi Driver*. You saw, experienced his isolation and understood *why* he acts irrationally and with violence.'

'Being famous isn't fun,' Scorsese went on to say. 'But you don't know that until you experience it.' After completion of *The King of Comedy* he had thoughts that he himself might be kidnapped. 'Or Bob. I didn't go out for a while.'

The assassination of singer John Lennon and the subsequent resurrection of Travis Bickle seemed to fortify a changing attitude about celebrity in general, and that may have cost *The King of Comedy* its theatrical life. Certainly the strangely upbeat ending where Rupert triumphs prompted a tirade from one major intellectual mouthpiece, the *New York Review of Books*. It castigated both director and star, saying, '*The King of Comedy* doesn't share a joke with the audience ... it makes the audience into dupes; if you laughed at Rupert's jokes, you made a criminal a star. And in raising the specter of the controversial *Taxi Driver* ending (in which Travis winds up an unlikely hero), it courts more anxiety, and more press maunderings about movie violence ...'

Most critics were lavish in their praise of De Niro's acting. The fault was he was almost too good at it in this picture. As one put it, 'Rupert is the nice nut, the dangerous devotee, the logical looney who can pop up at any moment with a grin, a gag or a gun.' De Niro felt this way too, saying, 'I think maybe the reason *The King of Comedy* wasn't well received was that it gave off an aura of something people didn't want to look at or know ... People react to what's projected,' and their reaction to Rupert was one of distaste and rejection. Whether it ever finds an audience remains to be seen.

De Niro didn't have time to mull over the picture's failure, however, as a project had finally come together that he'd been interested in for several years, Sergio Leone's Jewish gangster epic, *Once Upon A Time In America*.

Leone was the director who had brought Clint Eastwood to movie stardom in the mid-sixties via his Italian/Spanish 'spaghetti' westerns, *A Fistful of Dollars, For A Few Dollars More* and *The Good, The Bad and The Ugly*. Since their international success he had been able to entice bigger stars to his projects, particularly Henry Fonda in the well-received *Once Upon A Time In The West*. That film, made in 1966, *A Fistful of Dynamite* (1971) and now *Once Upon A Time In America* were meant to be a trilogy emphasizing Leone's love of things American, and he'd been working on putting this third one together for some ten years. Obsessed with American history, he would take this picture out of the Old West and into the gangster era that started in the twenties. In fact, he planned to span the generations from the twenties to the late sixties in telling his story, which he said would be a 'homage to the American films I love and to America itself'.

De Niro was rumoured to have been paid some $2 million and worked on the film sporadically for a year and a half as it wended its way through production in Rome, Venice, New York (where an entire city block was reconstructed), Paris and Toronto. Leone had wanted to work with him for some time, having considered him for a part in *Once Upon A Time In The West* some twelve years earlier. He'd been re-introduced to the actor by producer Arnon Milchan, who'd just worked with him in *The King of Comedy* and who was putting this film together as well.

When Leone asked Bobby's advice about casting the film, he was delighted. The pair worked easily together, and Leone was quick to accept his suggestion that all the principal actors play themselves – in their twenties, their fifties and their sixties – to make the film more realistic, and they eventually cast some eighty-eight speaking parts. The actors they signed up included James Woods in the pivotal role of Max, Elizabeth McGovern as Deborah, Tuesday Weld as Carol, Max's girl, Bobby's old pal Joe Pesci as Frankie, Treat Williams as fictional union leader Jimmy O'Donnell and Oscar-winner Louise Fletcher* as a madam.

Certainly Leone was thrilled at having De Niro's participation, telling *Sight and Sound*: 'De Niro has always been emblematic of realistic or even hyper-realistic cinema, and the way he and I have adapted to our reciprocal needs and personalities is exactly that something new which made me want all the more to have him in the leading role.' Bobby gave him ample proof of his hyper-realistic sense of acting when certain scenes ran up to fifty takes to complete, the most talked-about, perhaps, involving alarm clocks. At one point Bobby's character Noodles is awakened by one. When a retake was needed, Bobby wanted a new clock, and then several more so that he could continually register honest surprise in his reaction to its ringing!

Leone's films have always been plot-heavy – even *A Fistful of Dollars* was burdened with a subplot about a saviour figure amidst the shoot outs but he outdid even himself with *Once Upon A Time In America*. As fashioned in his mind and then put to film, the multi-generational story of five Jewish boys centres on the undying friendship between De Niro's Noodles and Woods' Max from the time they were boys on New York's Lower East Side in the early twenties. Elizabeth McGovern plays the girl of De Niro's dreams, while Tuesday Weld essays the role of Carol, Woods' moll, the quintessential double-dealing dame of every thirties gangster movie. Dozens of other characters weave their way into and out of these turbulent lives until, finally, only Noodles is left to remember how it was.

Leone's problems with the film could fill another book, but, in short, he made the same mistake De Niro's other native Italian director, Bernardo Bertolucci, made with *1900* – he shot too much footage to make a releasable and profitable movie. Leone may well have wanted to praise America and do it homage but,

---

* Don't bother looking for Louise Fletcher in any of the versions of the completed film: her part was totally cut out during initial editing. An expensive exercise in directing was that!

to start with, he should have first taken a course in the business of American film.

Through complicated financing and his own powerful vision, Leone shot and put together a film that was just over four hours long and which was rumoured to have cost between $30 and $40 million. Finding it wildly over-budget and length, Warner Bros, its American distributor, had a fit – and ironically it was some of Warners' own gangster epics of the thirties to which Leone was paying tribute. The Film Warners was expecting was to be 165 minutes long. Leone chopped his version down to 225 minutes but it was still too lengthy, and Warners decided to cut it themselves, trimming it down to 143 minutes. This version, stripped of Leone's most striking images and flashbacks, played to mostly empty theatres. The original-length film was marketed on two video cassettes and has proved to be a rental success.*

For all concerned, *Once Upon A Time In America* had been an expensive, sprawling gamble that didn't pay off. Certainly it did Leone no good, nor did it help his cavalcade of talent, particularly De Niro.

When the uncut version was shown at the Cannes Film Festival in 1984, European critics were quite lavish in their praises. Many women in the audience had quite a different reaction, however, when it came to De Niro's two rape scenes in the film, involving Tuesday Weld in one and Elizabeth McGovern in the other. After the screening an American woman walked up to him and screamed at him and Leone for these scenes of sexual violence, shouting, 'I was deeply embarrassed to be in the theatre. As a woman, I was demoralized.'

De Niro was dumbstruck at the criticism. While he knew the scenes had been explicitly brutal, he also realized they were integral to his character and therefore legitimate to the film. Now he was face to face with the possibility that he'd been wrong. Pulling a white cap down over his saddened eyes, he plunged into the crowd and disappeared. Back at the luxurious Hôtel du Cap in Cap d'Antibes, he went into seclusion until he

---

* When De Niro had his huge success as Al Capone in 1987's *The Untouchables*, yet another version of *Once Upon A Time …* surfaced on American coming in at 192 minutes. Shown in two parts by NBC, it was not the ratings-winner they were expecting, and this time the equation of De Niro plus gangsters proved a complete failure.

could quietly book himself on a plane for home. He was so affected by the woman's understandable tirade that from that moment on he did no more publicity for the film.

12 Falling in Love

With two mega-flops just behind him and his fortieth birthday just ahead, Bobby decided to try a new tack with his career, something totally new, yet a staple of the movie-star business: he made the move to become a romantic leading man. Insiders were quick to guess that he was doing so because his gallery of obsessed characters had driven his female audience away, and for once these pundits could have been right. After all, when most couples go to a movie the woman chooses, and what kind of woman would be attracted to the likes of Travis Bickle, Rupert Pupkin or Noodles Aaronsen?

True, the reviews of both *The King of Comedy* and the full-length *Once Upon A Time In America* were excellent, but what good are they when no one goes to see the picture? In short, De Niro was at the point of becoming one of those actors who can be guaranteed to give a sterling performance but who just isn't bankable. His salary per picture was now $2 million, but paying it wasn't any assurance that a built-in audience would necessarily follow. The Hollywood buzz was that he was fast becoming the victim of his own integrity, always choosing parts for their acting challenge rather than for personal popularity. They were right, but the word was out that he needed a mainstream hit, so he set out to find one.

Falling In Love seemed ideal, especially with all the positive energy going into it: New York City location shooting, a director Bobby knew and appreciated (Ulu Grosbard from *True Confessions*), Harvey Keitel to play his best friend and, finally, the current Screen Queen, Meryl Streep, as his leading lady. Ever since their pairing in *The Deer Hunter* six years before, Bobby said, 'I was always thinking of something I could do with Meryl – a play, a movie, anything.'

Meryl Streep's career had prospered wildly since their last

movie together. She'd followed it with a string of hits, including *The French Lieutenant's Woman. Kramer Vs. Kramer* and her Oscar-winning *Sophie's Choice*, and she had emerged as the screen's pre-eminent star/actress, able, in the eyes of fans and critics alike, to do just about anything. Also she was considered a very bankable name.

In choosing to become a contender in the 'romantic leading man' sweepstakes, De Niro would be fighting a losing battle as that screen genre had been in jeopardy for years. Paul Newman's longtime lead in the category was over and Robert Redford's was passing swiftly – more press appeal than mass appeal. Of the younger leading man, Richard Gere was currently the hottest but his characters were usually sexual desperadoes and hardly standard leading-man material.

Falling in Love presented De Niro with another challenge in that it *lacked* one, a reason for him to indulge his well-known penchant for research – from which he usually emerged totally disguised. To play Frank Raftis, an architectural engineer, about all he could do was study blueprints and get a macho haircut. 'I did some research on being a construction foreman,' he later said, 'but that didn't make my role any easier. I mean, he's not me.' (In the film there was really only one scene that showed his job, during which he shuffled papers and made some phone calls. Hardly the payoff he was used to getting from his character studies.)

No, this time De Niro had no false noses, added poundage or greying hair to hide behind: nor did his co-star. Like De Niro, Meryl Streep had used many an actor's trick during her career, particularly her talent in accents in *Sophie's Choice*. When she and De Niro had done *The Deer Hunter*, they were both still on the verge of popular stardom, whereas now the Oscars were well in place and it was their talent that sustained them. Script in hand, they spent long hours in Meryl's SoHo loft in Manhattan going over and over the script, looking for the special moments that would make it personal and believable to themselves. 'We wanted something real, something awkward and crumpled,' she later said.

That was just what these particular characters called for. Set in New York during a snowless Christmas season, *Falling In Love* is the story of two basically happy and married people from the suburbs who meet by chance in a crowded Fifth Avenue bookstore. They bump into each other and accidentally pick up each other's books; on Christmas morning he gives his wife a book on sailing, while she hands her husband one on the joys of gardening. This particular scene gives each star a chance to expose character, showing De Niro as a dutifully harnessed husband and father of two sons, while Meryl's the obviously unfulfilled wife of a doctor for whom she's given up her own career as a freelance commercial artist to make him the perfect suburban home.

Before that pivotal morning, though, there's an intriguing collage commenting on the isolation of city life as we see De Niro and Streep cross each other's path several times before they finally meet at Rizzoli's bookstore. On an escalator, she's going up while he's on the down side. They buy hotdogs from the same sidewalk vendor and at one point are speaking to their respective mates in side-by-side glass-walled telephone kiosks. It was obvious that camerman Peter Suschitzky shot these location scenes with a loving intensity for the city, making it look glossy and aloof with an almost winterish frost over his lens. (George Cukor's 1981 film *Rich and Famous* looked like a home movie, serving up dirty and dark boulevards, in comparison with *Falling In Love's* pale and clean ones. Not a few critics thought that *Rich and Famous* also served up a more believable story too.)

Three months later the pair meet again on the same commuter train and awkwardly recognize each other. He explains he's on his way to a construction site while she volunteers she's going to see her dying father, played by George Martin in a strikingly sympathetic portrait of a strong man being brought down by forces outside his control.

De Niro and Streep evoke a maturely warm chemistry together, with Meryl wisely using her streak of vulnerability to its greatest advantage. She shyly admits her attraction to Bobby in a series of quick, birdlike glances, her eyes wide with genuine surprise that such an unexpected romance should come into her stable and carefully ordered life.

De Niro approached his character with much the same sense of caution. Since his Frank Raftis is the happily married father of two beautiful little boys, his initial reaction to Streep's Molly is more of simple interest and wonderment that anything like this could ever happen to him at all. He doesn't see himself as a romantic man, let alone an unfaithful husband, and in one scene corners his pal Keitel in their gym and asks him if he thinks he's good-looking. Keitel only laughs, giving him no help or reassurance at all.

The sexual tension between Frank and Molly comes to a very slow boil as, at first, they're afraid even of acknowledging it, let alone consummating their emotions. Neither wants to threaten the present, even though they begin to realize that they've settled for life rather than holding out for something more. One of the main problems with the story, though, is that what they think they've settled for is more than most people ever get, so it's hard to work up much sympathy for them.

At the fever pitch of their relationship, Frank backs out, opts for a job in Denver and calls his erstwhile lover to say goodbye. He wants to see her one more time, but her husband intercepts the call and tells him no. Meanwhile, knowing he's leaving, she's trying to get to him, driving through wind and rain to reach the airport in time. She misses him. Eventually both marriages fall apart, but neither knows it and they're shown listlessly going through days until it's Christmas again and they meet by chance in the same bookstore where it all began the year before.

Each thinks the other ended the relationship, so it's an easy reunion. After a stiff and hesitant conversation, she says goodbye and leaves as the camera goes back to his face. We can see him decide he wants her and charge out onto Fifth Avenue to look for her, finally finding her on the same commuter train they'd taken so often in the past. Reminiscent of *Brief Encounter* and other forties films, *Falling In Love* ends on a twisting note. The two are together again but we have no real idea of what will happen next, and director Grosbard gives us no clearcut answer. Relying on the timeworn gimmick of the freeze frame which shows their happiness at rediscovering each other, the film ends. A cop-out? Most reviewers thought so, not to mention the public.

Not that the stars hadn't tried to make it work, especially De Niro in one of the lowest-keyed performances of his life. Who knows if his gamble might not have paid off had the story been more dramatic and the roles meatier? Publicity for the picture didn't help much, as it was touted as being 'the *Kramer Vs. Kramer* of 1984', a ludicrous comparison.

Still in the character of hardworking, mild-mannered Frank Raftis, De Niro helped to publicize the piece, a chore he usually avoided. In fact, it was for *Falling In Love* that he gave his first major interview in nearly a decade, to *Parade* magazine's Barbara Goldsmith. In it he waxed enthusiastic about the kind of life he wanted and what stardom and celebrity had brought him: 'I want freedom and a certain mobility, and I've arranged to have it. I live well. God knows I'm not complaining. Anyway, who has sympathy for the rich and famous? I don't. Why should anybody? I live better than I thought I'd ever live.'

When asked about his obsessive need for privacy, he replied, 'It's a choice you make. You can only experience so much fame. I don't know how people can live that way; they must get tired and bored with it. I want people to give me space.' When he is recognized, he admitted, 'There's an aura about me that says, "Back off." Usually people are nice. They understand that I relate to them on a one-to-one basis.'

What had celebrity given him? 'It lets me expand my work. I can do roles I want, with people I like. I don't have to work with anyone I don't like. I don't have to go below a certain level, and I can avoid a lot of problems … I guess there are other rewards. Small rewards. You get a good table at restaurants. Very small.'

His surprisingly congenial candour was almost as if the character from *Falling In Love* had stepped off the screen and into real life. His Method Acting was carried into Method Interviewing, and he let just enough of himself show through to appear vulnerable and human, yet able to maintain a personal distance at the same time.

As for the film, it was a charming exercise in naturalness for both its high-powered stars. Stripped of accents and outrageous histrionics, Meryl never looked lovelier or acted more realistically. And it proved that putty noses and poundage weren't necessities for De Niro to make a character come alive. As Frank Raftis, he came across as warm, earthy and raffishly attractive, so much so, in fact, that it might have been the film's undoing. De Niro fans looking for the wham-bam punch of a *Raging Bull* or the deranged intensity of a *Taxi Driver* were disappointed. Streep fans too must have walked away shaking their heads if they went looking for another character in her gallery of extreme on-screen personalities. If anything, *Falling In Love* was for the true *aficionado* because it was an opportunity to see both stars playing roles as close to themselves as they're ever likely to again.

Bobby must have been suffering from an uneasy conscience over the way he'd dropped out of promoting *Once Upon A Time In America*, because when its producer, Arnon Milchan, asked him to be in his new film, he said yes. The brainchild of former *Monty Python* regular Terry Gilliam, the film was to be called *Brazil*, and the best thing about it turned out to be its lushly recorded title song.

Since his rise to stardom, Bobby had never done a cameo role, but he did in this one, labouring hard to make sense of a scrabbled script and inept direction. A *cause célèbre* long before its release because of studio-director squabbles, the end result, though heralded by some, was one long and confusing bore. Set in the supposedly not-so-distant future, *Brazil* has been described as an 'Orwellian pantomime' with its story of an ordinary man caught in a society where he is dwarfed by the machinery he's invented to simplify his life. Star Jonathan Pryce wanders through this labyrinth of unfriendly technology like a man caught in a post-nuclear nightmare.

Financed by Universal Pictures, Gilliam's ideas were fleshed out in the heavy company of Tom Stoppard and Charles McKeown, and hopes were high that a comic romp in the style of the *Python* pictures was in the offing. Instead there emerged a tale of a socially inept bureaucrat caught in a world where the sound of an electric typewriter seems like a lurking enemy and the buzzing of the refrigerator an omen of nasty things to come.

Naturally the only people with any true power in this society are the repairmen – of whom De Niro is one. Actually, since he operates outside Central Services, the Big Brother of Gilliam's future, he's a renegade repairman who comes to Pryce's rescue. Literally popping out of Pryce's office wall, it's a remarkable screen entrance but doesn't lead to much, although he imbued the role with the energy of a young Errol Flynn. Eventually the system catches up with De Niro's Harry Tuttle, and he's literally buried in a sea of newspapers which symbolize the paperwork of a militant bureaucracy.

Gilliam's satiric fantasy was a costly one – some $15 million at least – and Universal was not pleased. Once again De Niro had involved himself in a controversial project filmed by a headstrong, undisciplined director, and the film languished in various cutting-rooms, not to mention trade headlines, for some time before finally seen. Critics were wildly divided at the results, the most enthusiastic being those belonging to the Los Angeles Film Critics Association, who voted it the Best Picture of 1985. Many others found it pointless and boring, an overblown and unendingly gloomy view of the world for those unfortunate to live long enough to become a part of this 'new order'. Reviewers also wondered just why De Niro had lent his awesome presence to such an outing but the only explanation forthcoming was that he'd long been an admirer of *Monty Python* and company and had wanted a chance to work with Terry Gilliam.

By this time he'd acquired several addresses, including the house in California, an apartment in Rome and a lavish loft in the regentrified section of New York City called TriBeCa, but nowhere seemed really home to him. His personal life remained a mysterious blank, and while there was no divorce from Diahnne, he was never photographed with anyone else. Perhaps it was the barometer of his fame at that time that he wasn't hounded by photographers and star-watchers, since, to be blunt, his public image was then at a low point. The gamble for classic stardom had failed with *Falling In Love*, and his more exotic roles had not paid off.

Bobby's experiences in Britain during the filming of *Brazil* had given him a new respect for the British, and when director Roland Joffe approached him about a new film, he was interested. Joffe had won an Oscar nomination for his 1984 film *The Killing Fields*, and this new venture promised to be every bit as exciting. The producer would be *Killing Fields*' David Puttnam, and his enthusiasm was equally great: '*The Mission* is a Clint Eastwood version of *Beckett*, an intellectual theme treated with guts.' Those words would be sweet music to any actor's ears but were especially melodious to De Niro's. Another interesting point would be that, if he took the part in the film, he'd be playing opposite a man of almost equal stature in the acting world, Jeremy Irons, the handsome Englishman who had shot to stardom opposite Meryl Streep in *The French Lieutenant's Woman*.

Joffe wooed De Niro once he'd made up his mind he wanted him. 'Bobby was the first person I thought of for the role,' he said. 'But then I thought, "No, come on, there must be other people" ... and I looked around a lot, but in the end I realized my first instinct was the right one. There wasn't anybody who had the inner complexity that Bob had. Most other actors who approached the role tended to have to work at it. The extraordinary thing about Bob is that the inner complexity is there without him having to do anything – it's a part of his presence.' And the part Joffe wanted De Niro to play, that of Mendoza, the grubbily bearded slave-trader-turned-priest, would require a complex talent of a finely tuned nature. Also the film would be shot completely on location in Colombia and Argentina, a challenge De Niro had never taken up before but which might have its own, if occasionally questionable, advantages. As Joffe would later say, 'I've heard that shooting in studio here in Hollywood has its own dangers. Of the two jungles, the real jungle may be the more comfortable.'

He was quick to invite Bobby to visit the proposed location sites as a learning experience for them both, saying, 'If you're interested in the film, come and see the kind of world in which it is set. And let me have a chance to look at you in that world.' Bobby agreed and during the trip had a chance to have long conversations with Joffe, eventually reaching the decision that he wanted to be a part of this special and isolated world. He got to see first-hand the remarkably tight-knit atmosphere that develops when shooting in the wild, the sense of family and dedication to the work that such an atmosphere enforces and nurtures. Joffe said of that period, 'For the director and actor it is very important. It's your first date.'

De Niro had a good time on the date and was shortly signed for the gruelling film that would mean over three months spent in South America, where he would evolve yet again into another personality. 'Bob De Niro actually changed,' said the director. 'His look changed. In three days of walking about with the Colombian men and observing their ways, the New York Italian began to disappear and a powerful Hispanic appeared.'

13   The Mission-*ary*

The Mission was a far cry from the historical tableaux that Hollywood had produced under the aegis of Cecil B. De Mille. De Mille stars, such as Charlton Heston and Hedy Lamarr, playing Moses and Delilah, had never ventured farther afield than Paramount Studio's backlot when they were emoting, but nitty-gritty realism was never that director's aim when depicting the past. In the eighties, it was assumed that the public wanted no more of perfumed palaces built on opulent sets but preferred instead the mud and murk of the real thing – which Roland Joffe was determined to give them in his sprawling tale of love, death and religion set in the mid-1700s in South America.

With a script that had been lovingly written by Robert Bolt, the Academy-award-winning screenwriter of *Doctor Zhivago* and *A Man For All Seasons*, Joffe and producer Puttnam set out to tell the story of the Jesuit missions in South America following the signing of the Treaty of Madrid in 1750 and the subsequent bloodbath between the Spanish and the Guarani Indians.

Bolt's script centred on two powerful male roles, that of Mendoza, to be played by De Niro, and Jeremy Irons' saintly Father Gabriel. It opens with a quietly startling sequence as we see a priest tethered to a cross being set adrift on a river. Gradually the current increases and the human cargo moves more rapidly down through the frothy water until, in a breathtaking moment, it's carried over and down the mammoth Iguazu Falls. Above these falls live the Guaranis, and this act symbolizes their rejection of the Catholic faith.

Downstream, Father Gabriel receives this graphic message but isn't about to take no for an answer and sets out painfully to climb the falls and convert the Indians. This he does through the mystery and magic of music, playing an oboe to the natives, which curiously wins them over. His next step is to begin building a mission for them.

As a counterpoint to Gabriel's religious endeavours, we meet the dastardly Mendoza, a mercenary and slave-trader whose only interest in these Indians is to capture them and sell them into slavery. He is filled with thoughts of a young woman of the town of Cartagena with whom he's desperately in love. This girl, in turn, is already in love with Mendoza's younger brother, Felipe, played by Aidan Quinn, a youth whom Mendoza has sponsored and has had brought up more gently than himself, thanks to his slave-trade earnings. When Mendoza finds out the true object of Carlotta's affections, he is filled with a black rage and a desire to strike out. While trying to explain the situation, Felipe is drawn into a duel with his brother and is killed by him. Alone now, Mendoza is awash with guilty remorse and renounces his lifestyle to seek redemption with the Jesuits.

Gabriel sets a heavy penance for Mendoza, one that he has to continue until he truly forgives himself. It begins with his symbolically scaling the slippery and dangerous sides of the Iguazu Falls, dragging the heavy load of his mercenary's armour behind him. It's only when he's reached the top of the precipice and is received with warmth by the Indians he'd previously hunted that his guilt is expiated. Seeing that he's finally forgiven himself, Gabriel accepts him as a novice in the Jesuit order, and Mendoza becomes a born-again man of action.

Almost as soon as Mendoza's conversion is complete comes word that a papal emissary is *en route* from Portugal to evaluate the missions and decide whether they will continue or be ceded to Spain as a result of the Treaty of Madrid – in which case the converted Indians would all be up for grabs.

After his evaluation, Cardinal Altamirano (richly played by Irish character actor Ray McAnally) decrees that the missions will be disbanded. Gabriel reacts to this order with reverent defiance while Mendoza reverts to his war-like habits and tried to unite the Indians to defeat the intruding Spanish soldiers. It's a doomed cause, and the Indians are quickly slaughtered and the missions burned in a gorgeously photographed scene of carnage which also sees the deaths of Gabriel and Mendoza.

A relatively simple story, it was to unfold on an epic canvas with the aid of top talent on all sides. But it shortly proved not to be such an easy task to do it.

The Iguazu waterfalls define the present-day borders of Brazil, Paraguay and Argentina, and it was there that production was set up for three of the sixteen weeks of filming. Local Indians, some 350 members of the Wuanana tribe, were hired to portray the doomed Guaranis. They had a problem, though, because when the cast and crew first showed up dressed uniformly in jeans, T-shirts and snakeproof boots, the Indians, were at a loss as to just who was the most important. In the end, it came down to beards. Those who had them were important, those who didn't were not. Since the two stars, De Niro and Irons, director Joffe, producer Puttnam and the director of cinematography, Chris Menges, all wore beards, the system worked as well as any.

The Indians were also quick to recognize that De Niro was the most important of them all. He was now deeply into character as the renegade-turned-priest, and they could tell this by the sense of awe he inspired in the rest of the cast and crew and by the way he avoided people's eyes. On the set he was 'Mr De Niro' to most people, 'Robert' to some, 'Bob' to a few, and 'Bobby' to only the most privileged. The Indians thought him some unknown god, an opinion only half-jokingly seconded by Puttnam. 'Bobby is exactly like them,' he said. 'They believe that when you take a photograph of a man you remove something. Bobby feels that about press photographs and interviews.'

Joffe was more admiring of his star as De Niro kept exploring the skin of Mendoza the warrior. 'There was little research he could do, in practical terms, as he was playing an eighteenth-century mercenary; which is why I think this was such an interesting part for Bob. He had to create off his imagination .... Bobby worked every day on his fencing, and our fencing maestro was amazed by Bobby's progress. Bobby needed to feel that if he *had* a sword he could kill somebody with it. He could have held his own with anybody in a duel. He also learned to ride those high-stepping Spanish horses, and read all the books available on the subject of the film.'

Walled into his new screen personality, De Niro fortified his isolation by willingly having two armed guards around him twenty-four hours a day, keeping watch outside his hotel room, on the set and everywhere else he ventured. Anyone visiting the set who asked about these elaborate precautions was told they were ordered by the film's insurance company, who feared he might be kidnapped, not an idle consideration considering the locale.

Jeremy Irons seemed a bit more accessible, most likely because he was glad to be working. After having a major success on Broadway starring in *The Real Thing*, he'd found subsequent movie offers a bit thin. He told reporter Douglas Heay that, 'Everyone gets offers of bad pictures but in the year before we came here I'd read only two good scripts – *Out of Africa* and *The Mission*. I just wanted to be aboard.'

But being 'aboard' didn't mean an easy ride, for the sixteen long weeks in remote locations were, according to Puttnam, 'sheer hell'. At one time or another everyone on the film – with the exception of De Niro – came down with varying degrees of amoebic dysentery and had to deal with other forces of nature and South America life as well.

One of the principal sets for the picture, Father Gabriel's San Carlos mission above the falls, was accidentally built in a site chosen by Joffe that was squarely on a major drug-smuggling route – a fact not realized until the huge church built of mud, mango poles and thatch was firmly in place, along with the surrounding Indian village. While the Government of Colombia was enthusiastic and cooperative about having this giant film project in their country, 'The Colombians who worked with us on the ground didn't care what Bogotá had decided and there were moments that were utterly impossible.' Since it was too late to move the set and still meet their schedule, the cast and crew had to get used to having armed Colombian troops constantly on patrol. No wonder De Niro needed security!

The weather was equally uncooperative and they had to battle torrential downpours, blistering humidity in 110° heat, and floods that at one time threatened the only bridge out of the remote location area. And the kidnapping theory concerning De Niro was not that far-fetched as, at times, remote stretches of road linking the location and the crew's fortress-like hotel were invaded by bands of small boys who pulled ropes taut across the road as cars approached, thinking to stop them and force the occupants to give them money.

Even the climactic scene of the film almost turned into a life-and-death situation. When the San Carlos mission was burned for the finale, its construction materials caused it to go up faster than anticipated. The giant church quickly disintegrated and the fire swept through the schoolroom and adjoining huts, forcing the camera crew to beat a very hasty retreat, virtually grabbing their cameras and equipment on their way as the fire came close to getting out of control. When watching the film, one can see that the pain and surprise on many of the faces of the extras were very real but, thankfully, there were only a few minor injuries.

Since a film industry is practically non-existent in Colombia, virtually everything needed for the production had to be flown in from somewhere else: cameras, lights, all of it. These items ranged from the exotic (some 660 wigs and hairpieces shipped over from Rome) to the mundane (salad-dressing and tea shipped from Britain for the crew). A small zoo had to be constructed to house armadillos, spider monkeys and crocodiles needed for the shoot, as well as a huge set for the below-the-falls mission made of plaster. Although it was not built to last, the owner of the land on which it stood requested that it be left standing so he could use it as a tourist attraction.

The Indian extras were paid some $75,000 for their work, most of which went into a specially established community fund for later use. Unfortunately the food was all bought locally – except for that salad-dressing and tea – which proved a large oversight as, had that too been imported, the widespread food-poisoning that plagued both cast and crew might have been avoided.

One major problem that Joffe had to deal with immediately was the diversity of his two male leads, as it became quickly apparent to him that they were very different types as actors, each needing a special directorial insight. He told *American Film*: 'It was very interesting because they come from two totally different traditions. Jeremy's immediate concern in a scene would be: "How do I look? Where am I going to be? How will the lights strike me? What character will I present when I'm on the screen?" And a lot of our discussions were aimed at preventing him from having a preconceived image of the scene. I did everything I could to make him feel that the *image* he created didn't matter, that it was what came from the inside.

'Now where Jeremy works from outside in, Bob works from the inside out. He's an extraordinary man, a real artist. I have enormous respect for him because he makes artist's choices. He'll risk anything, he'll do anything in any order, because he's listening for the voice. So you give him time; you allow him to discover where he's going. You allow the scene to develop. The problem, of course, is how do they work together? Because they are actually going in different directions. There is no answer to that at all, except to pray that you get them to meet about halfway.'

Irons later added: 'Bob is a private man, so it takes a long time to get to know him. He is a man obsessed with his work and who continually worries. It got easier, and we eventually trusted each other ... It took us a little while to come together and realize we were actually working in the same way. But I think Bob is a lovely man.' Originally Irons' Father Gabriel was meant to be played by a much older actor, but Joffe had decided that the dramatic tension between the two main characters would be heightened if they were about the same age, thus making Mendoza/De Niro's acceptance of Gabriel's penance even more piercing since it comes from a contemporary instead of a revered elder.

As a director, Joffe was frankly thrilled with what Bobby was bringing to the screen, especially admiring his ability to toss his ego aside and dive as deeply as he could into his character. The street gladiator of *Taxi Driver* and the fighting instincts of the *Raging Bull* were combined in his Mendoza. 'The Mission was a very courageous step for Bobby to take,' he later said, 'a very proper one – and I'm glad he's done it. Mendoza was a classical role, and nobody until now had the balls and size to tackle it. But I felt Bobby would rise to that. And he did.' He continued, 'As an actor, Bobby was very generous. He worked with all the other actors to prepare for their roles; there was no sense of the "star" on set.'

As for De Niro the man, Joffe was less successful in getting to know that part of him. 'He is very guarded, although I found him warm and personable. But I think it is very sane of Bob to hold back a part of himself in a working relationship. Of himself, an actor should give eighty per cent, and twenty per cent he should guard. You have to feel that there is a part of you where a director's sticky fingers haven't pried. It is important for a performer to keep a sense of himself. You give up a lot as an actor, and Bob especially gives an enormous amount to the films he's in. So he most definitely needs his privacy. He has earned it.'

The Mission ended up coming in over budget with a whopping cost of $22 million, but hopes were equally high that it was worth it. Sensing it had a Class A product on its hands, the film's distributor, Warner Bros, decided to open it slowly and, hopefully, let word of mouth build it into a hit.*

In New York City the film opened at the prestigious Cinema 1 theatre 'in the tradition of Warner Bros', most distinguished films' and managed to gross more in its first week than either *The Killing Fields* or *Chariots of Fire*, their previous 'artistic' hits. Irons, Joffe and Puttnam hit the publicity trail to hype the film but De Niro's awesome figure was absent; notably so.

With the rise of the television movie critics during the eighties came an increasing number of newscast audience surveys, almost like the 'preview cards' that were filled in by audiences during the thirties and forties. Television reporters would stick a microphone in a patron's face as he was leaving the cinema and ask for a quick opinion, and right from the start audiences expressed doubts about the success of *The Mission*.

Most of these ticket-buying pundits in New York City – where everyone's a critic – found the acting of De Niro and Irons first rate, but the film seemed overlong and the story sluggish. One woman went so far in her few seconds of television fame as to suggest that some forty-five minutes could easily have been clipped from the middle of the film because they 'really dragged'. In retrospect, though, the opinions of many of these instant critics were not far from those offered by the professionals.

The Mission had one big plus going for it as it went into US release, and that was the fact that in May 1986 it had been voted the Palme d'Or as the best picture shown in contention at the Cannes Film Festival, winning the coveted prize over films including Britain's *Mona Lisa*, Italy's lavish *Otello*, starring Placido Domingo, and writer Sam Shephard's *Fool for Love*.

Coming so soon after the Libyan incident in which American bombers had accidentally shelled Kaddafi's home outside Tripoli and killed his daughter, concern was high that the

* For comparison's sake, this was a far cry from the way in which showman De Mille would open his historical extravaganzas. Since Paramount still owned its own chain of theatres until the early fifties, he'd open his pictures in their major film palaces and then into wider release in the neighbourhood theatres. Eventually they would filter down to the double-bills. In those pre-cassette days the film got its major saturation – and major grosses – on its first run but the double-bill, and later a major re-issue, would bring additional money into the studio's coffers. Re-issues today are all but gone, with the exception of Walt Disney's perennial animated classics, which have proved to be money in the bank.

festival might be used as a site for attention-getting revenge, and so most American stars didn't attend. De Niro stayed at home, as did most others with films in competition, including Sylvester Stallone and directors Steven Spielberg and Martin Scorsese. The biggest American 'name' to show up was Eric Roberts, there to hype his picture *Runaway Train*. The no-shows didn't seem to affect either the business or the pleasure of the sun-drenched festival, which came off without any apparent hitch. (De Niro's friend Scorsese won the Best Director award for his black comedy *After Hours*. Its star, Griffin Dunne, accepted it in his place.)

American critics were shortly divided over the merits of *The Mission*, Palme d'Or or not, with opinions varying from Gene Shalit's 'a magnificent achievement!' to *People* magazine's tabbing it 'a ponderous mess with a misplaced reverence for the Hollywood cliché'.

With his long, greasy hair and beard scattered with grey, De Niro was found to make a menacing villain, bringing, according to *The Hollywood Reporter*, '...a fierce strength to his role, and he does it with steely aplomb; however, as written, it is a character who transforms too abruptly'.

Oddly enough, it was the New York critics who seemed most harsh on him, almost as if their favourite native movie hooligan had somehow disgraced them with his conversion to the other side. *The Post*'s Stephen Silverman called the picture '...pretentious hokum .... De Niro gives the first truly embarrassing performance of his career', while the *Times* shook their critical finger with 'Mr De Niro, who was very fine as the street-wise priest in *True Confessions*, is all right here until he opens his mouth. His New York accent doesn't easily fit.'

Nit-picker extraordinaire Rex Reed sang a different tune, gushing that it was '...a great adventure for moviegoers! Great acting and spectacular cinematography make it a movie worth seeing.' *Newsweek*'s Jack Kroll, a longtime De Niro supporter, also had superlatives to toss around, calling it '...a sweeping spectacle! Dynamic! Explosive! ... Joffe and his actors score some stunning achievements. A stupendous true story.' No reviewer could resist the opening sequence, though, and the Iguazu Falls received more good publicity than Niagara.

Screenwriter Robert Bolt's script received good-to-great notices, and he was honoured for it in Los Angeles by the

Writers' Guild of America. That was especially heart-warming for him, as just six years before, after undergoing open-heart surgery, he'd suffered a massive stroke and this film was by way of being his comeback. Bolt was quick to say that his painfully slow but steady recovery was due largely to the devoted attentions of his ex-wife, actress Sarah Miles. Two years before he'd suffered that physical bodyblow he'd first seen the Iguazu Falls, and the idea of telling the story of the Treaty of Madrid and its consequences had first surfaced. After that visit he was inspired. 'Three times the size of Niagara, you know – and I said "Well we've got to do a film about them, haven't we?"'

As always, the public were the ultimate critic, and in the case of *The Mission* they generally turned thumbs down. The film eventually chalked up American grosses of $17.2 million – barely half enough needed to break even. Despite its lack of big box-office, though, it remains a memorable credit on De Niro's list of films, combining, as it does, both challenge and prestige. Unfortunately, along with that top billing he received in it came responsibility for the picture's fate in the eyes of movie-producers. No American ones were coming up with anything interesting, so De Niro continued to focus his attention on London-based film-makers.

14 *De Niro Goes to the Devil!*

The saucy tabloids of Great Britain have never been known to let any celebrity off easy – and few have captured their interest as much as the reclusive De Niro.

Late in 1985, for example, *The Sun* headlined a story in which an exotic black fashion model named Gillian de Terville proclaimed, 'I'M ROBERT DE NIRO'S BLACK BEAUTY!', complete with details about what she professed to be their eighteen-month-long affaire. One of the paper's notorious Page 3 Girls, Gillian, breathlessly told of the passion, the pain and the pleasure of being a De Niro consort.

According to her story, De Niro took one look at her photograph and was so interested that he tracked her down through a producer friend to a semi-detached house in South London that she shared with her family. Recalling a moment as romantic as an early scene from *Raging Bull*, she told how she first heard from him while 'I was washing my car.' Her mother answered the phone.

'I went to the phone and I could hear this American accent and I said I didn't know anyone called Bob. He said, "You know, Robert De Niro." We'd never met, but he managed to convince me that it was him. He said he'd seen my picture and wanted to take me out for dinner.'

Gillian said she agreed to meet with him for a drink at his hotel but on the appointed day found herself overtired from an assignment and almost ready to skip the engagement. 'I had been lugging all my clothes around, my hair was dirty and my face thick with greasy make-up. But when I rang his hotel to cancel because I looked so rough, he begged me to come anyway. And now I'm really glad I turned up. We hit it off straight away,' and she left thinking, 'He'd seen me at my worst, so I could only get better.'

It obviously did, as the twenty-four-year-old was soon talking about spending time in New York with him, presumably in his modern loft in the TriBeCa section of Manhattan. 'I love staying there. It's a big place with lots of paintings, huge windows and a big round king-sized bed. There are all sorts of gadgets in the headboard – for the radio, TV and that sort of thing.' Feeling she was on a publicity streak, Gillian kept referring to the bed – 'There's even a switch to heat things up. Once I woke up in the middle of the night absolutely roasting. I said: "Robert, we're overheating." The bed was much too hot and he had to turn it down.'

Gillian seemed primed for a major romance as she rhapsodized about the possibilities, signalled by De Niro's attentiveness. 'He's very romantic and always holds my hand or puts his arm round me.'

'Robert is very much the strong silent type. He hates publicity and he's not flash. But sometimes we do go out with other stars. The other night we went to Tramp, the top London Club. We shared a table with Joan Collins and Christopher Walken and there was me – little Gillian sitting in the middle.'

'Little Gillian' went on to talk of more of her New York adventures: 'He took me to a Yoko Ono party in New York. I was all dressed up in a black dinner suit with lots of diamonds and pearls. Suddenly, the lights came on and all the photographers pointed their cameras at me. I thought, this is it – my chance for superstardom. Then I realized they were all snapping Yoko, who was standing just behind me.' So much for Gillian's ambitions for media attention on De Niro's arm, and while she also said that, 'Often we just go out for a quiet dinner,' it's unlikely it would have been to any paparazzi-haunted place, considering De Niro's deep need for personal privacy. Even if they had, he had long been developing a trick originated by Woody Allen of leaving a restaurant alone, with his date coming out a few minutes before or after.

At the time of *The Sun* interview Gillian also commented on how quickly he'd been accepted by her family: 'He's been round quite a few times. He arrives in a cab and sits on the sofa and watches TV with the rest of the family. He gets on well with my dad and my 18-year-old brother .... I don't think the neighbours even know it's him.'

That was no wonder, as at the time he must have been

preparing for *The Mission* and, 'Recently he's grown his hair and a beard for his latest film. When I saw him I didn't realise it *was* him for a minute. I don't like his new look but Robert does – because it meant we could walk around the streets of New York without anyone recognizing us.'

According to Gillian, the attraction she felt for him was amply returned. 'I like him very much. When we're apart he phones me at home all the time and tells me he wants me to be with him.'

When queried about who was picking up the tab for all this partying, Gillian was quick to give an answer: 'We have a proper relationship and we have a lot of fun together [but] I wouldn't like anyone to think he was whirling me around and paying for everything. It's not like that with me and Robert. Sometimes he pays my air fare because, obviously, he does have a lot of money, but that's all.' She was also able to be objective about her situation and its future: 'We haven't discussed marriage. We're just enjoying ourselves. There's so much I want to do before I even think of anything like that.'

Gillian did confess to liking '...expensive things – I have been known to spend £250 on a pair of shoes. But often I go out in old clothes. Robert said to me once, "For God's sake – are those the only shoes you've got?" ... I've been sitting in restaurants and seen girls quite openly flaunting and trying to get off with Robert under my nose. I just laugh.'

Apparently Robert had the last laugh though, as after baring her soul to the popular press there's no evidence that the super-shy superstar ever contacted her again, even when he was back in London meeting Alan Parker to discuss *Angel Heart*. Going public, as she had, would have put the final nail in the coffin of that supposed romance.

If anything, De Niro probably laughed off these romantic revelations, realizing that they did his image as a hot star no harm at all with his fans. In fact, they made him appear less remote and more humanly vulnerable – personality traits that certainly would not be evident in his forthcoming *Angel Heart*, as in that he would be virtually going to the devil!

After playing the warrior-turned-priest, Mendoza, this role would be very different, and he was so much intrigued with it that, for the first time since reaching major stardom, he sacrificed top billing. He felt he didn't need or perhaps deserve it, as the part was a virtual cameo role, albeit a pivotal one in Parker's steamy tale of murder, sex and supernatural horror. Fresh though that challenge was, he did not immediately agree to do it. Said Parker, 'He is constantly taking risks. It was an enormous risk for him to accept a supporting role in *Angel Heart*. And I admire him for taking it. But although it's a small role, it took him three months to agree to do it. He never says yes to anything immediately, he just asks questions. He has to consider each role carefully, because he has such a special career at stake. And he has made so few mistakes in that career. To accept *Angel Heart* was a very brave decision. And I think he'll surprise people.'

De Niro was a bit more pragmatic about it all when he later spoke to *Rolling Stone*, readily admitting that the size of the part really didn't matter because it was frankly the best thing around. 'Nothing had come along that seemed right, and I liked the idea of doing a cameo too. It's fun. You do these kinds of bigger-than-life-type parts or characters – mythic almost. I don't know what people's perceptions were, but the main thing is you have to do it for yourself. Please other people, and that's good, but if not, what are you gonna do?'

Parker knew just what to do once Bobby was signed and delivered. An interesting director, he'd once vowed to work in every genre of film before he died, and *Angel Heart* clearly took him into a new category. Initially, Parker's reputation had come from the sociological thriller *Midnight Express* in 1978, followed two years later by the acclaimed musical *Fame*. In 1981 he'd directed Albert Finney and Diane Keaton in *Shoot the Moon*, a romantic melodrama, and after that a concert film, *Pink Floyd – The Wall*. *Angel Heart*, said critic Roger Ebert, would let him chalk off two more genres in one – the private eye thriller and the horror movie, or, as *The Hollywood Reporter* would later call it, 'a blend of mean streets and the nether world'.

The private eye, in this case, was to be played by Mickey Rourke, an actor of some repute who'd made his first screen impression in a small part in the William Hurt–Kathleen Turner scorcher *Body Heat*. Since then he'd turned a few more new faces to the camera in *Diner* (1982), *The Pope of Greenwich Village* (1984) and the critically lambasted sex drama *9½ weeks*. His reputation for diversity and raw talent had many people calling him Hollywood's hottest new actor, and a few 'the new De Niro'.

Normally a star would hate working with someone being dubbed a 'new' version of himself, but De Niro welcomed the challenge. Short, overweight and hardly a love god, Rourke had an ample behind which would later prove too much for film censors.

Rourke plays Harry Angel, a down-at-heel detective who in 1955 is grateful for a $50-a-day job tracking down a long-missing crooner named Johnny Favorite. Angel's office was recreated on New York City Lower East Side and the street also doubled for a Harlem exterior where he first meets his new employer, Louis Cyphre (say it fast!).

For De Niro this was yet another return to his old neighbourhood and, as for *Mean Streets*, *The Godfather Part II*, *The Gang That Couldn't Shoot Straight* and *Taxi Driver*, the local Chamber of Commerce should have given him a medal for bringing money into the community. The production people redecorated an entire block of Elridge Street to recreate it as a mid-fifties locale. Parking-meters were taken out, old street-lamps brought in and entire shop fronts changed back in time along with appropriate prices. One unsuspecting butcher was suddenly besieged with customers demanding the chickens advertised in his window as going for 25 cents a pound! He solaced them by explaining the situation and then letting them be corralled to serve as extras in the movie. They didn't get their bargain chicken but they did get to be movie stars for a day, and paid ones at that.

When Angel meets Cyphre for the first ime, in a Harlem temple (shown quickly and gruesomely to be the den of voodoo fanatics), he thinks he's been chosen for this missing-persons job because his name begins with A and is therefore easy to find in the phone book. He couldn't be more wrong but doesn't know that as he sets out to find the lost singer. It seems Favorite has left an unpaid dept to Cyphre, and he wants to know if he's dead or alive so he can collect.

The clumsy Angel, looking like a rumpled bed and operating out of an office that one writer said looked like a gift to charity from Sam Spade, sets forth on a journey into a nightmare land that could be barely imagined by the most restless sleeper on the hottest of nights.

Following a lead given him by Cyphre, Angel goes to an upstate New York sanatorium where the singer was last known to reside, as a shell-shocked war victim, which leads him to a morphine-addicted doctor who ends up dead after telling him that Favorite had been taken away years before by a man and young woman – down south, the doctor recalls, as Angel teases the information out of him by holding back his drugs.

On Cyphre's urging, after they meet in an Italian restaurant where he promises him an extra $5,000, Angel follows the trail to New Orleans, where he locates Favorite's ex-girlfriend, Margaret Krusemark, played by the elegant Lauren Bacall-lookalike Charlotte Rampling. She refuses to help him, and he then tracks down the mulatto daughter of another of Johnny's women, Epiphany Proudfoot, who he finds out is Johnny's daughter to boot. Through Epiphany and Toots Sweet, an ageing guitarist from Favorite's old band, Angel is slowly introduced into a world of voodoo and violence.

Harry follows Toots Sweet one night from his seedy nightclub to a voodoo ceremony in the bayous where he's shocked to see Epiphany as the priestess, letting the blood of a freshly killed chicken wash down over her face and body before she couples wildly in the dirt with one of the young men. Toots and Margaret also end up mutilated and very dead, and Harry seeks out Epiphany for solace, climaxing in a sex scene that had censors howling as they make abandoned love in Harry's cheap hotel room, where the walls begin to drip blood. The nudity was both natural and gravely unsettling at the same time.

Then Cyphre turns up in New Orleans and meets his detective in the back of the church, taking cynical caution to quiet his confused employee when Angel uses profanity to point out the corner he's been backed into, with dead bodies surfacing all around his investigations. De Niro is quite believably evil and frightening in this screen incarnation: his black-clad body is immaculately clad, his fingernails elegantly pointed and his long hair carefully clipped back in a ponytail which mades his bearded face all the more obviously diabolical. Unfortunately Harry's now too befuddled to notice.

The closer Angel gets to finding Johnny Favorite, the nearer he also gets to losing himself. Margaret's father gives him the final key to the puzzle, telling him that he and his daughter had worked with the singer to disguise his soul, already promised to the Devil in return for his stardom, by taking over the body of a young soldier they'd picked up in Times Square twelve years before. The soldier's dogtags had been kept by Margaret in a sealed vase. Angel breaks into her apartment, finds and smashes the vase and finds the dogtags – with his own name on them.

In a spin of horrified disbelief, he turns to find Cyphre sitting in the living-room, his hair now undone and flowing around his shoulders, and listens in stupefied disbelief as Lou Cyphre – Lucifer – tells him his own story and fate: he's the one who has murdered all those people, the doctor, Margaret, Toots Sweet ...

Running out, Angel returns to his hotel to find the police in his room standing over the dead Epiphany, who is sprawled in blood across his bed. 'That's your gun up her snatch,' growls one detective. Suddenly Harry can't avoid the truth any longer and admits it is. 'You'll burn for this,' the cop continues. 'I know, ' Harry mumbles in reply. 'In hell.' The film ends with Harry in a squeaky warehouse lift ... going down and down and down.

Knowing De Niro's penchant for researching a part, many people wondered how he'd done it this time, how he'd managed to go to the devil. Parker was quick to reply, 'Oh, but he *has* researched the role. There isn't any aspect of the character he hasn't examined minutely – from his fingernails to his eyes to his hair. The amount of detail he is putting into Louis Cyphre is phenomenal. His is both a physical and intellectual approach, a *complete* approach to characterization. I've never met an actor who put so much into a part, and such a small part at that.'

By this point Parker was done with the film and recovering from the demands of its stars, particularly De Niro. 'I'm not sure I could work with him on an entire film. It would be too much of an exhausting experience. I think Roland Joffe would agree with me, from what he's told me. De Niro would constantly ask questions on the set, and then ring me up every day with new possibilities and ideas. His involvement was phenomenal, sheerly phenomenal.'

What turned into a public phenomenon about *Angel Heart*, though, was Lisa Bonet's no-holds-barred portrayal of the voodoo princess, Epiphany Proudfoot. Just eighteen, the remarkably seductive girl showed sides and angles of herself that had never been displayed on television, where she reigned as Bill Cosby's virginal daughter on *The Cosby Show*. The spunky, spaniel-eyed actress was anxious to make the transition from television to movie star, but no one expected the storm of controversy she would stir up on the way. Just named one of the ten most beautiful women in America by *Harper's Bazaar* magazine (along with the likes of Nancy Reagan, Cybill Shepherd and Priscilla Presley), she was fast becoming the country's best-loved teenager when she signed to make her film début. Her television image was drastically in contrast to her part as Epiphany, and the press jumped on the story when the news first surfaced that she'd be showing herself nude on the screen entangled with Mickey Rourke.

Supposedly she'd checked this out with Bill Cosby beforehand, to have him say, 'Take it. It will be good for your career.' But when the picture was finished and edited – and found deserving of an X-rating for its sexual content – his people said Lisa hadn't told him just how explicit her part would require her to be.

Director Parker acknowledged that the scenes in question were even sexier than those Mickey had played in the also-controversial but little-seen *9½ Weeks* with Kim Basinger. 'Our scene was a little less coy, and consequently, Mickey was naked for the first time in his career. Lisa was more relaxed than he was. In fact, she was a lot more relaxed than all of us and took it very coolly.' That scene, with the blood splattering down the walls and onto the orgasmic bodies of the two stars was so explicit that Parker shot it with barest minimum of crew – just four, with Lisa and Mickey downing bottles of Japanese beer to help them get into the proper mood of abandonment. The pair became so comfortably relaxed that, before long, they were 'utterly oblivious to our presence'.

For her part, Lisa was happy at having the chance to make the film at all. She told *The Star*, 'I know it's hard for a lot of actresses who play kids in shows to make the jump into adult roles …. For me the transition to a meatier part had come so early, it's really exciting. I'm doing it for the first time, and I know it won't hurt my image. I put my faith in Alan Parker to let me do everything with taste. But what can I lose? I'm in my first movie with Mickey Rourke and Robert De Niro. I can't lose.'

The faith that Parker inspired in the youngster reflected his own attitudes towards actors. When *American Film* queried him about his working habits, he had this to say: 'The most important thing is to create an atmosphere of trust, where if we – myself and the crew – are at our bests, then perhaps the actors will be too. No director ever got a performance from an actor that wasn't there to begin with. Some actors require a lot of attention in talking about a role, like Robert De Niro, for instance. He's an extremely controlled actor, extraordinarily professional, and his questions are many and varied, but always helpful.'

However sincere the efforts going in, the resulting movie can hardly be called a fun-filled trip to the cinema. Instead, it turned out to be one of the gloomiest pictures of the year, despite its polish and talent. The mid-eighties had seen a box-office rebirth of *film noir* suspense thrillers, such as *Against All Odds, Jagged Edge, No Mercy* and *The Big Easy. Angel Heart* was supposed to join this list of money-makers, mixing, as it did, the popular ingredients of a down-at-heel investigator, mysterious woman and shocking violence, plus in this case the Devil as well, into a potent movie cocktail, but the dark, foreboding aspects of this ornately complex thriller kept it from its expected box-office fizz.

Even the ongoing controversy over Lisa Bonet's nudity didn't help it to succeed, and, possibly, may have hastened its demise at the ticket windows. Her mainstream audience was either too young or too shocked to see it. Through careful pruning, including the excising of 'ten seconds of Mickey Rourke's rump', Parker brought the film below the X-rated level, but one writer was quick to point out that, 'By casting Little Miss Black Innocence in such a raunchy role, Parker had practically violated a national shrine.'

Imaginative? To be sure. Provocative? Absolutely. Popular? Alas, no. Filled with the unsettled logic of a terrible dream, people just weren't interested in experiencing all that while still willingly awake!

De Niro, almost as if in keeping with his devilish character, was notably quiet during the weeks of newspaper controversy that swirled around his latest film, smart enough to realize that the picture would either prove itself or not. As with other films before this, he felt he'd contributed as much of himself as possible and had been honest to both his art and his talent with this ultimate stretch of characterization and then letting it go. Reviewers were uniformly in awe of his continuing display of acting versatility – this person on the screen reeks of evil! – but one can also see he had a good time playing the part.

In the main, horror pictures usually spelled out the waning days of a film career coupled with smaller billing and much smaller money, but De Niro was perceived as being a major star who'd simply decided to explore the genre because the script was good and the time seemed right. The fact that the released version was considered watered down because the censors clipped some of Rourke's rear and Bonet's breasts mattered little to him, for he'd proved what he'd wanted to prove by just making the film. He'd explored evil before in many films, and he didn't lament the early demise of this definition of it.

Evil comes in many guises, and yet another one shortly came his way that was strong enough to make him do something he'd wanted to do for a long time – return to the live excitement of performing on the New York stage.

After thirteen years, there had been a lot of professional water under the bridge of De Niro's career since he'd appeared in the Manhattan Theatre Club production of Julie Bovasso's *Schubert's Last Serenade*. Recently he had seen the commercial failure of three films in a row, *Falling In Love*, *The Mission* and now *Angel Heart*. He needed to return to the roots of his career, the nurturing-ground of the talent that had made him millions, and made him world famous.

Joseph Papp, the noted director of New York City's Public Theater and a major force in the stage world of the 1970s and eighties had an answer. Papp was the man who'd brought New York theatre back to life after the lacklustre Broadway offerings of previous years had nearly killed it. He'd sponsored the Theater in the Park which had helped the careers of Meryl Streep and Kevin Kline among many others. He was also on the lookout for writing talent, and when he read a script by a previously unproduced writer named Reinaldo Povod, he was quick to forward it to De Niro. De Niro was a bit sceptical until he read it. Titled *Cuba And His Teddy Bear*, it was the gritty story of a drug-dealer and his teenage son and seemed just the ticket to bring De Niro again before the public eye. Joe Papp was happily astonished when he quickly said yes.

He signed with Papp for a limited run of eight weeks at Papp's Public Theater in downtown New York, but once the announcement was made, pandemonium took over at the box-office. People may not have been eager to see him on screen as the Devil but they clamoured to see him in person.

In Britain the great film stars are often seen lighting up West End theatres and national touring companies, presenting both

Robert Duvall, the cop, and De Niro, the priest, share a quiet
moment in *True Confessions*. The gritty story of personal greed
versus religion was a critical hit for both actors, and gave De Niro
his second chance to wear priestly garb on screen.

De Niro's Rupert Pupkin in a fantasy sequence from *The King of
Comedy*. Here he imagines himself as a personal friend of
superstar Jerry Langford (Jerry Lewis). The pair never socialized
off the set.

De Niro adds his input to a scene in *Falling in Love* as co-star Meryl Streep and director Ulu Grosbard pay close attention. For virtually the first time in their careers, the stars were playing 'ordinary people' – perhaps the reason the film wasn't the success it deserved to be.

Meryl Streep and De Niro as the ill-fated lovers in *Falling in Love*. A studio portrait emphasizes the hero's wedding ring in this contemporary drama of delicate infidelity.

A mud-caked De Niro, as Mendoza, experiences forgiveness with Jeremy Irons' Father Gabriel in *The Mission*.

Fatly ferocious, De Niro as Al Capone tries to stare down his enemies. *The Untouchables* was his most popular movie in years.

For the first time in his career as a major star, De Niro looks
exactly like himself in the comedy hit *Midnight Run*.

classics and the *avant garde* in plays. Maggie Smith, Derek Jacobi, Glenda Jackson and others are to be constantly found on the legitimate stage as a means of expanding and defining their talent. Across the water in the US, though, the stage had also spawned many great careers, from Spencer Tracy and Katherine Hepburn to Dustin Hoffman and Meryl Streep, but few returned to it on a regular basis. To most, Broadway success was simply a launching-pad where they could poise to soar westwards to Hollywood, the land of big houses and bigger bucks. Far too few of the younger generation had bothered to make the trip back unless they had to.

Al Pacino is an exception, and so is De Niro. He'd never denied that he missed the stage, telling a London interviewer once, 'I haven't been on the stage in ten years. There seems to be no time. But I'd like to do a play ... I'm looking for plays.'

Once he had finished reading *Cuba And His Teddy Bear*, he realized he need look no further. Oddly enough, the playwright had written *Cuba* ... with De Niro in mind as the violent drug-dealer father who tries to steer his son's life in a healthier direction. Povod had briefly met De Niro when he was a child and Bobby was filming *Taxi Driver* on the Lower East Side – home turf to them both. Once he met the actor again, he was more impressed than ever, telling *People* magazine, 'He's more concerned about you than he is about himself .... He's changed my attitude towards people.' And those were attitudes that needed changing, as Povod had previously had a drug addiction that almost killed him. Of his mentor, the late writer Miguel Pinero, he said, 'I wanted to become him. So I became addicted to drugs when I was 19 – till I was 22.' Pinero died of drugs at a young age.

Povod's seven character play focuses on a drug-dealer, De Niro, and his teenage son, and mirrors the playwright's relationship with his own Cuban-born father. 'I was born and raised on 13th Street on the Lower East Side. This was a story I'd been working on since I was 22; when I was 25, it clicked.' The gut-gripping drama was admittedly autobiographical. 'I'm the kid, Teddy – when I was young I was chubby, like a teddy bear – and my father was Cuba [pronounced Cooba], a street-fighting man. It's ironic that the fruits of Cuba's labor, his drugs, become Teddy's fruit. But it's really a play about father and son. Drugs are the vehicle to bring them together.'

To play Teddy, Papp engaged teen idol Ralph Macchio. Fresh from his successes in *The Karate Kid I* and *II* and *The Outsiders*, he too was looking for a change from the big screen. 'That Hollywood stuff can drive you crazy,' he told *People*. 'All that merchandising – the dolls, the posters, making sure the MTV video is out a month before the release – it all turns movies into a mumble-jumble of commerciality. I wanted to get away from that and really do some acting.'

In the difficult role of the son who's alternatively attracted and repelled by the drug world of his father, Cuba, the young star was able to hold his own against the De Niro powerhouse. 'The play is an ensemble work but Mr De Niro is the center of it, and he's different every night. That's why it's such a wonderful experience for me. He's taught me that acting is limitless; you can go any place you want with it, any direction.'

De Niro attacked his role as the dealer/dad with streetwise relish, sporting the pigtailed long hair, beard and moustache from *Angel Heart* and parading all the dormant stage-acting tricks he'd learned in his youth. It was obviously an uncomfortable subject for audiences to live with for two straight hours, and the reviews were indeed mixed, with several speculating that without his presence in it the play probably would have never been produced. What they didn't know, however, was that the lure of seeing De Niro live would send ticket-buyers into a frenzy. The limited run was quickly sold out for its entire length, with touts making a bundle. Papp replied to the demand by setting up a television monitor in a room adjacent to the theatre and charging $7 a head for live closed-circuit 'simulcasts'.

After negotiating the time (money wasn't the object, as De Niro and company were working for minimum), Papp convinced him to take the show to Broadway, and they opened there at the Longacre Theater on 16 July 1986, where it was scheduled to run until 21 September. That production was De Niro's official Broadway début after some eighteen years as an actor.

Robert Osborne of *The Hollywood Reporter* noted the following day that the play was not only selling out again but '...also causing the kind of "star" excitement appeal that used to be a Broadway staple. They line up behind police barricades just to watch De Niro and Macchio enter the theater at 7.30 p.m.'

De Niro spent as much time with his children as possible, slowly introducing them into his real world and not the nightmare one he was living in on stage every night. When Martin Scorsese and Liza Minelli hosted a tribute to Liza's late father, director Vincente Minelli, at New York's Museum of Modern Art, he showed up with a lovely young girl on his arm – his now eighteen-year-old stepdaughter, nicknamed Drina. They spent the evening mingling with the likes of Tom Cruise and Mimi Rogers, Candice Bergen, Andy Warhol and Yoko Ono.

Just the night before he'd attended a cast party for the *Cuba* company at which his son, Raphael, appeared with his mother Diahnne. As the party wound down, Diahnne left with several girlfriends while Bobby quietly took his son home. Though distinctly separated and living their own lives, Bobby and Diahnne remained friends.

An interesting aspect of De Niro's personality as a star is that he's never sold his celebrity cheaply. While, in effect, he might give it away when he took the *Cuba* company to Riker's Island to perform the show for prison inmates, he'd worked too hard to gain it to have it tarnished for a quick buck.

An interesting phenomenon began in the early to mid-eighties when Japanese television commercial-makers began to employ American stars to advertise their products on their home screens. Many big names who had refused to make commercials for the US market quite happily succumbed to the big-money temptations from abroad where their regular fans would never see them. John Travolta, among others, accepted six-figure fees to endorse various Japanese beverages. When Asahi Beer decided to look for a star – a rugged image-setter – to plug their product, they approached De Niro. He turned them down, as did Al Pacino and then Sam Shepard. Finally they got through to Mel Gibson, a beer-drinker from way back, who was signed to swig the product for the Japanese television audiences.

Friendship counted for much with De Niro too, even if it occasionally brought back unhappy memories. When Robin Williams sold out the Metropolitan Opera House two nights running to tape a television special, Bobby was on hand. Having himself worked through the troubles that drug-use can bring, Williams was now making jokes about it. 'Cocaine, what a wonderful drug!' he enthused from the stage. 'Anything that makes you paranoid and impotent – mmm, give me some of *that!'* The laughs came long and hard in the star-studded audience that included Sean Penn and Madonna, but in his seventh-row seat De Niro must have recalled with sadness how cocaine had taken the life of their friend John Belushi.

The success of *Cuba And His Teddy Bear* seemed to have revitalized him, and De Niro seemed more outgoing, showing up at various New York parties happily sprouting his *Angel Heart/Cuba* beard and hair. He must have known he wouldn't be wearing it for long.

During the run of the play, another old friend had resurfaced in De Niro's life, director Brian De Palma. De Palma had a new film in the works, and it promised to be a blockbuster. It was *The Untouchables*, and he wanted De Niro to be in it. And not just any role, mind you – certainly one of the most demanding of his career, for De Palma wanted Bobby to portray a man of such mythic power and violence that he would put Vito Corleone in the shade. De Palma wanted Bobby to play the most famous, most *in*famous gangster of them all – Al Capone.

15   *The Ultimate 'Al'*

De Niro was instantly interested in playing Al Capone, but there were problems. He'd also been offered, and was considering, the male lead in *Ironweed*, which promised to reunite him with Meryl Streep, and there was the continuing success of his play to be dealt with.

Brian walked away thinking that he couldn't get him. *Cuba* ... was such a hit that it seemed its run would run over into his production time, and so, with stoic resignation, he signed up another actor to play the part, for a very respectable $200,000. That actor was Bob Hoskins, a gutsy little British actor who'd recently been praised for his role in the critically acclaimed *Mona Lisa*. Said Hoskins, 'He was quite straight with me. I met him in Los Angeles and he said: "I really want Robert De Niro but if he doesn't do it will you?" It was just a small part, two weeks work in Chicago, and the money was good so I said, "Yes." I had no contract or anything. What really surprised me was that after De Niro decided to do it, De Palma insisted on paying me – even though he didn't owe me a penny. I couldn't believe it. It's the easiest $200,000 I never earned. If all acting was like that I might have started earlier.'

After agreeing to the job, Hoskins took his family on holiday to Yugoslavia, planning to join *The Untouchables* later in Chicago, but once there he heard that De Niro had become available and would be taking the role. Hoskins' agent swallowed the news, cashed the very respectable cheque that was forthcoming and said, 'I don't think it will hurt his career because I have seventeen film offers right now for Bob.'

Though De Niro liked David Mamet's script, there was still the question of time. Besides finishing the Broadway run of his play, he wanted enough of it to pack on the thirty pounds which he felt were necessary to flesh himself out for the character of the burly gangster. 'He's concerned about the shape of his face for the part,' De Palma said. There was also the matter of his salary, rumoured to be $2 million for two weeks' work. Producer Art Linson felt that the schedule slowdown and salary demands might still scuttle De Niro's participation – 'The delay would have cost us about $2 million on top of his salary' – but, happily, a compromise was reached. De Niro would get his asked-for salary but there would be no delay in shooting. Instead he'd arrive in Chicago on 27 October, and all his scenes would be shot during the last days of production.

True, the part of Al Capone was basically another cameo for De Niro, but his sense of commitment didn't end just because the script pages were fewer. After flying to Chicago for a brief costume session, he took off for Italy where, in just the few weeks between the end of *Cuba* ... and the shooting of *The Untouchables*, he planned on eating his way back up the scales. A publicist for the film later joked that, 'We tried to tell him there's good restaurants in Chicago, but he disappeared.'

Once ensconced in Italy, Bobby had research to do, as well as eating. (One tabloid breathlessly reported that he'd taken the precaution of carting along four cases of canned food with him because he was afraid the nuclear disaster at Chernobyl the preceding spring might have tainted the pasta and he didn't want to take any chances of going hungry.) With him he had all the books written about Capone, copies of the four films in which he'd already been featured, and newsreels of the Prohibition period.

When he finally did show up in Chicago, the transformation was startling. Though he was far from being the grotesque shape he'd made of himself to play Jake La Motta, it was obvious that his eating time had not been spent in vain. Once fitted in his costumes – which included silk boxer shorts, silk pyjamas, shirts and a maroon monogramed silk brocade robe from Sulka, such as the real Capone had worn – and make-up, even De Palma was open-mouthed in awe. Art Linson was equally impressed and determined to make the change work for the picture by keeping his star hidden. 'I don't want to see any photos of him in makeup,' he decreed. 'I don't want to see him in any of the coming attractions trailers. I want the same sense of mystery that surrounded Brando in *The Godfather*.' Linson planned to exploit this new look to the hilt, and who could blame him? For

$2 million, you should get to call a few of the important shots.

Just mentioning *The Godfather*, however, brought up the inevitable argument that has plagued most gangster movies – namely, that they romanticize crime. Not this one, De Palma said quickly. 'This is a film about good and evil, and my point of view is clear. These criminals are evil, they wreak havoc with other people's lives, and should be put away. In all my films, good triumphs over evil.' And the period depicted in the film was a time of intense evil.

In 1931 Prohibition (the ban on the manufacture, sale and consumption of alcoholic drinks) was the law of the land, but Al Capone is the king of Chicago. His influence stretches to the mayor's office and the police department and he controls all the racketeering in town, be it bootleg booze, gambling or girls. Capone considers himself in control of, if not above, the law, and his crime empire is a multi-million-dollar business. The Government wants him stopped and, seeing no help coming from the city's nominal heads, sends Treasury agent Eliot Ness to do it. Ness and his few chosen lieutenants – 'the Untouchables' – work towards Capone's downfall.

With a powerhouse script by Tony Award-winning play-wright David Mamet and with a director like Brian De Palma, the stage – or rather screen – was set for some grand performing, and no one was disappointed. *The Los Angeles Times'* Peter Rainer was later to call the ensuing stew of violence and eventual triumph of the good guys De Palma's 'hallucinatory, operatic dream' and, for certain, he let all the stops out to make it that.

He was prepared to get his cast to do the same, especially the young leading man, Kevin Costner, who brought Eliot Ness to wide-screen life. (Originally there was talk that Mel Gibson was to play the part but he had to pass because of delays in production on his *Lethal Weapon*. If true, the delay worked to De Palma's advantage as Costner was perfect for Ness.)

Up until then, the thirty-two-year-old actor was best known for his gunslinger role in *Silverado*, a western that was supposed to rejuvenate that genre but didn't, and as the suicide centrepiece of *The Big Chill*, in which his part was totally cut out except for shots of his hands as an undertaker dresses his body. 'I have kind of a quiet career,' he said. 'It may be the quietest career in Hollywood.'

De Niro and Linson believed that Costner's quality of strength was what they wanted and came up with a simple solution to compensate for his lack of name value. 'There was no doubt in my mind that Kevin was the best for it,' Linson said. 'I wanted him as soon as I saw *Silverado* .... Paramount was nervous: Kevin wasn't famous. So what we did was surround him with people who were, in particular De Niro and Sean Connery.'

Costner delved into researching Ness's life with some of the passion De Niro was using for his role, studying Chicago sites from which the gangsters had operated, pondering old newspapers and books about Chicago in the thirties and even listening to the recollections of the widow of a former Capone lieutenant. When it was time for gun-training, he took some lessons from an eighty-eight-year-old who was one of the original Untouchables.

Many people wondered if the film would be anything like the successful early-sixties television show of the same name, which had starred Robert Stack, but David Mamet was quick to put them straight: 'The movie is intended to be a drama, not just an entertainment. This is not a homage to the TV show, which I liked very much. But the TV show was more Ness versus Capone and his men; the film is more about the innocent young agent and the old Irish policeman who teaches him how to become a cop.'

For that important character, De Palma had picked Sean Connery, the erstwhile James Bond. It turned out to be an inspired piece of casting as the strength of Connery's Jamie Malone perfectly complemented the initial idealism of Costner's Ness. Said De Palma of Kevin's appeal: 'He has the straight-arrow idealism of a young Jimmy Stewart. Very vulnerable. A lot of people who read our script said "But you haven't made Ness strong enough." They missed the whole point. This isn't Dirty Harry .... This is a portrait of a man coming of age. He wants to get Capone. But he wants to get him within the law.' He was also optimistic about Costner's screen charm, especially in the light of the failure of his brutal *Scarface* in 1983. 'Women didn't go for *Scarface* and Al Pacino's character in it. But Kevin has such humanity that he's attractive to women.'

But it was Capone's character that was the cornerstone of the story. De Palma was clearly intrigued by the charisma of the dead gangster, as was David Mamet, who used some of Capone's actual words in the movie's dialogue. 'What people forget,' Brian De Palma said, 'is that Al was a very popular guy. Ness was enforcing Prohibition that wasn't popular. Al was bringing people what they wanted – booze.

'And he was a charmer, the only gangster ever to give press conferences. That's pretty unusual, right? There's a funny speech he gave when he was in jail for tax evasion. He said, "I was a public benefactor and this is what you do to me. OK, now get your own liquor." Unfortunately we couldn't fit it in.'

To work in the press-conference angle, De Palma opened the picture with one, angling his camera down from the ceiling, focused on a barber's chair in which Capone is sprawled, being worked on by a barber, manicurist and bootblack while around him buzz a group of British reporters. We get the overpowering sense that Capone is the King Bee in this particular hive around which all else swarms and moves at his command. As the camera comes down closer to his towel-covered face, it's suddenly taken away and we see his face for the first time in full-screen close-up. With his hairline shaved back and thinned out and his face bulky with fat, lips drawn down at the corners, De Niro is unrecognizable once again, totally submerged in Capone.

He jokes with the reporters, talking down to them and, naturally, admitting to nothing. 'There is violence in Chicago, of course,' he placates them. 'But not by me and not by anyone I employ because it's not good business.'

When Eliot Ness comes to town full of optimistic zeal for law enforcement, the naïve Treasury agent tries to work within the graft-ridden police system of the city, but to humiliating defeat. Walking alone one night after a front-paged blunder that's made him a laughing-stock in the department, he meets an old patrolman walking his beat. The man's name is Jamie Malone, and he's the first honest cop Ness has met.

Soon he seeks out Malone for advice on stopping Capone, and the two join forces, with Malone – in a back church pew for privacy – telling Ness that, if he goes after the mobster, he must go all the way. 'Want to get Capone? Here's how you get him. He pulls a knife, you pull a gun. He sends one of yours to the hospital, you send one of his to the morgue. *That's* the Chicago way, and that's how you'll get Capone.'

The pair are shortly joined by a bespectacled Treasury Department bookkeeper, played by Charles Martin Smith, and a young rookie policeman, Andy Garcia, and the four of them are quickly dubbed 'the Untouchables' because they cannot be bought off.

Malone shows Ness where to find a huge cache of liquor – just across the street from the police station, in fact – and they raid the place, arresting the men inside, including a Capone lieutenant. When he hears of this, Capone erupts into a volcano of rage and plans a way to keep it from happening again.

At a large, round, impeccably set table, the tuxedo-clad mobster is surrounded by his closest allies. Suddenly he launches into a speech about his love for baseball, grabs a bat and walks around the table behind his men, declaring that teamwork is what's necessary for the baseball field and for life. 'Teamwork', he stresses over and over, until he's behind the man whose warehouse had been raided by the Untouchables. Suddenly he swings the bat up and then slams it down on the man's head, time and again, until the camera pulls back and we see the blood flowing across the table and very dead pulp of his skull. His henchmen watch with astonished eyes as they grasp this lesson that to stay on Capone's team means beating the Untouchables. It's a short but incredibly powerful scene which makes Capone seem larger than life and more than a match for Ness and company.

Eventually Ness has to pack his pregnant wife and young daughter off into hiding, and then he's on a plane with his men to intercept a shipment of bootleg hootch crossing the Canadian border. When they succeed again, Capone is thrown into another fit of fury, almost hysterical with anger, shouting, 'I want that son-of-a-bitch! … I want him *dead*! I want his family *dead*! I want his house burned to the *ground*! I want to go there in the middle of the night and piss on his ashes!'

Observing De Niro turning Capone into a savage animal harnessed into Armani suits, De Palma let him cut loose, standing back in awe. 'He's not Bob De Niro playing Capone. He *is* Capone … the weight helps, of course, so does the scar he wears (a souvenir from Capone's youth when he was a member of a Brooklyn gang) and he has a nose piece and his hairline is shaved back, but it all works.'

David Mamet, who'd won his Tony for *Glengarry Glen Ross*,

also helped with his sparse dialogue that cut quickly to the essence of the character and allowed De Niro's awesome physicality and sense of perverse bluster to take it from there.

When Capone's executioner, Frank Nitti (played with appropriate iciness by Billy Drago), kills Smith's character, Oscar Wallace, Ness storms into Capone's hotel to confront him. This was one of the beautifully blended scenes that mixed the real Chicago in with the film, as it was shot in the gaudy lobby of the old Balaban & Katz Theater which doubled for Capone's Hotel Lexington. Other touches of authenticity were Louis Sullivan's Auditorium Hotel, and the Rookery, remodelled by Frank Lloyd Wright in 1907, which served as police headquarters. The Tiffany-domed Chicago Public Library came into service, doubling as the courthouse where Capone's ultimately brought to trial.

Unchanged terraced houses were also used in the picture, particularly for Malone's apartment building where, in true De Palma bloodiness, he is machine-gunned down by Nitti just after he's retrieved the information needed to apprehend Capone's bookkeeper. (Ironically, for all his mayhem and murder, Capone was convicted, finally, only for tax evasion.) Ness arrives at Malone's too late to save his mentor but gets the information and, with the last Untouchable (Andy Garcia), sets out to get him.

Learning the accountant is leaving on a midnight train to Miami, the pair stake out Chicago's massive Union Station. At the same time De Palma cuts to Frank Nitti leaning over and whispering to Capone that Malone is dead. Capone is regally ensconced in his opera box, listening, face tear-streaked, to *I Pagliacci*. His face twists into a sour grimace of triumph as the tears continue running down his cheeks.

Back at the shadow-stained station, Ness and Stone wait it out, jumping at every sound and suspicious of every step. From Ness's vantage-point he can see the entrance to the platforms but looking down he also sees a young mother struggling to pull a pram up the long stairway leading to them, slowly moving first the suitcases and then the pram up and up. He moves to help her and, as he gets the pram to the top of the stairs, the gangsters appear with the bookkeeper in their midst. Ness starts to shoot, the pram slips away and, in painful slow motion, the shootout begins as it rolls to the edge and then starts bouncing down the stairs.

The baby is saved and the bookkeeper captured, but not until after one of the most violently excruciating scenes in film history – and all from an idea that wasn't even De Palma's! He was quick to give credit where it was due, though – to Sergei Eisenstein and his 1925 masterpiece *The Battleship Potemkin*. 'I haven't seen *Potemkin* in what – 25 years? But that famous scene on the Odessa steps [which also involved a pram] has always stayed with me. And it works beautifully in our movie.'

After finishing his work on the picture, De Niro withdrew to the seclusion of his loft in the TriBeCa section of New York City. A neighbourhood on the lower west side, it was the new SoHo, an area formerly filled with small factories which had, in the 1980s been made over into spacious condominiums with high ceilings and plenty of windows – and lots of privacy. Working out with weights in his private gym, he started dropping the Capone weight. While sweating through it, he also made a resolution to himself: that he was reaching an age where he had to stop punishing his body with huge gains and losses; it was becoming too much of a bothersome strain. By the time he was invited back to Hollywood for Paramount's seventy-fifth anniversary just after the New Year of 1987, he looked remarkably well.

When he got there, the early buzz on *The Untouchables* was that it was going to be a smash hit. Paramount, the studio who'd be releasing it, proved their faith in Bobby by making sure he was front and centre in their anniversary photo session on the Hollywood backlot. When *Life* magazine's cover story on the event came out, he had the prime position in the centre of the cover, surrounded by the other stars. There was no question that he deserved his position but what people asked when the issue hit news-stands was just why was Faye Dunaway also featured so prominently. After all, her last Paramount film, the laughable *Mommie Dearest*, had been a failure at the box-office and had practically killed her career overnight, sending her scuttling over to Britain for a wan remake of the classic *The Wicked lady*. It began to make more sense, though, when the cover photo was credited to her estranged husband, photographer Terry O'Neill.

The inside spread that featured De Niro in two thoughtfully provocative poses with Elizabeth Taylor seemed to punctuate Paramount's enthusiasm. While Elizabeth Taylor had never been a Paramount star (with the exception of her taking over *Elephant Walk* from an ailing Vivien Leigh in 1954), just her presence brought a sense of timelessness to the project – past meeting present, or film history in the making? The second of the two photos had her arm outstretched, hand resting on his shoulder, and it seemed almost a confirmation of film immortality, this most famous of actresses giving this most renowned actor her blessing. And perhaps the impetus for some smart producer to find a project they could do together!

In fact, talk of that, only not of a one-to-one screen relationship, surfaced shortly with reports that Italian director Franco Zeffirelli was preparing a $170 million version of *The Bible* in which he hoped to star Brando as Moses, Elizabeth Taylor as Mary Magdalene and De Niro, Peter O'Toole and Meryl Streep in as yet unnamed roles.

As a press release it sounded great, if wildly optimistic, and reminded film buffs of Irwin Allen's campy mid-fifties classic, *The Story of Mankind*, in which appeared just such an array of then-famous stars: Hedy Lamarr as Joan of Arc, Virginia Mayo as Cleopatra, Vincent Price as the Devil, Groucho Marx as Peter Minuet (who purchased Manhattan Island from the Indians) and Dennis Hopper as Napoleon to Marie Windsor's Josephine. Would that Taylor and De Niro had been announced for a new *Brief Encounter*, putting a fresh spin on that romantic tale. Or David Lean's *Hobson's Choice*. Or Hepburn's *Summertime*. Or any decent script that would test and cement these two great stars and bring out their personal bests. Hopefully it might still happen.

One story that was bandied about for De Niro was *Big*, about a young boy who suddenly finds himself in a thirty-five-year-old body. De Niro's friend Penny Marshall was to direct it, but he had trouble envisioning himself in the part, and the film was eventually made starring Tom Hanks – becoming one of the biggest moneymakers of 1988. As a 'Tom Hanks comedy', the story works beautifully; as a De Niro acting job, one can only wonder to what lengths he might have gone becoming a child again.

What seemed a much more likely offering was a script entitled *Handsome*, about an ugly man who's sent to prison, where he volunteers for some experimental plastic surgery. The operations are successful and he's transformed into a gorgeous man who then slips back into society with his new identity and appearance to seek revenge on the people who'd had him gaoled in the first place. De Niro's name was bandied around for this, as was Richard Gere's and John Travolta's, yet a finished film has never surfaced on this intriguing idea.

When the fledgling American Museum of the Moving Image planned to honour Elia Kazan early in 1987, there was a veritable avalanche of seldom-seen personalities on hand to participate. Party recluses such as Al Pacino and Dustin Hoffman were there, joining Tom Cruise, Eva Marie Saint, Norman Mailer and others in this evening in honour of 'The Godfather of directing'. De Niro was grateful to Kazan for the patience and inspiration he'd shown during the making of *The Last Tycoon* some years before, and it was a tribute to his friendship that, while the film had not been a success, Kazan's genius had not dimmed in his eyes.

The industry buzz on *The Untouchables* continued being both strong and positive, so when De Niro was asked to attend the opening-night gala of the Cannes Film Festival, he thought it wise to do so. The 1987 Festival was an affair vastly different from that of the preceding year. Security was noticeably less than before, when the fear of Libyan terrorist reprisals against Americans had put the town on red alert, and now many wanted to make the most of it.

It was the fortieth anniversary of the festival, and that fact added extra heat to the event that turned the town into the movie capital of the world for a few days every year. The event was so hot that this one brought out the Prince and Princess of Wales, but even their lustre was almost secondary to the parade of movie royalty that flocked to the Croisette.

On opening night it was Elizabeth Taylor, on the arm of temporary consort George Hamilton, who stole the spotlight from stars that included Joanne Woodward and Paul Newman, Mel Gibson, Bo and John Derek, Lillian Gish, John Travolta and De Niro, who'd flown in on Concorde just for the evening. At one point during the lavish reception, the Princess's brother, Viscount Althorp, himself a freelance reporter for American television, tried to collar De Niro for a private interview but he was quickly hustled out of the party by a security guard.

De Niro must have taken that as a warning of the way in which other reporters would be acting, as he was quickly back on a plane and headed home from this now-you-see-him, now-you-don't visit, though not before attaining his objective. Enough pictures had been taken to be splashed across European newspapers – along with the name of his latest film, *The Untouchables*.

16 A Hit and A Miss!

When publicity on *The Untouchables* began in earnest, De Niro had little choice but to grin and bear it, most notably on NBC-TV's *Today Show*. One of the conditions was that he wouldn't have to face the media alone, so Brian De Palma was with him, and together they answered questions and almost seemed to be enjoying it.

The movie scene that spring was a crowded one, and several stars who usually didn't publicize a picture were out in force; there was a lot of competition for box-office dollars. At Columbia, hopes were riding high on the Dustin Hoffman-Warren Beatty *Ishtar*, a mammothly expensive comedy (some $45 million) directed by Elaine May. Since the film had been rumoured to be in trouble, its two publicity-shy stars were more than willing to give television interviews (albeit shot in a studio with proper lighting and sound, so Beatty could look his youngest). They readily talked to magazines as well, and all this coverage prompted De Niro and De Palma to do a limited version for their film.

Naturally the first question out of the box was about how hard it was to handle an actor of De Niro's temperament, with Brian replying that it was 'not tough at all'. Asked the same about his director, Bobby was a bit more forthcoming: 'Oh, Brian's terrific. He's always been. This is, I think, the fourth movie we've done together and he's terrific. He's very easy and he's a great audience. He's *too* good sometimes. He laughs too much at stuff and makes you feel that it's better than you think it is.' Asked to describe De Palma in one word, he chose '...jovial. That's *one* word; there's many others I can think of.'

Asked the same question about his star, De Palma answered, 'Chameleon. And that's absolutely a compliment. What I've found so remarkable about Bobby and his performances, and became sort of a character in *Hi, Mom*, was his ability not only to become the person he's playing but to physically change the way he looks so that you don't recognize him from part to part. This is quite unique in a film actor because most stars are a persona. Here's a great film actor who suddenly becomes this other person and he is like a star in the visage of another human being, whether it be Al Capone or Jake La Motta or Travis Bickle.'

This intensity of characterization had had the advantage that, as De Niro was able to admit, he wasn't bothered a lot by autograph hounds. Just the question, though, brought up memories of Travis Bickle and the Reagan assassination attempt, and his answer was guarded: 'Sometimes people come over and ask me for an autograph and most of the time I'll do it. I won't when people ask you to repeat a line or something from a movie they know you by.' He didn't want to repeat the line but did admit the movie was usually *Taxi Driver*.

He was looking casually handsome in an open-necked sports shirt and brown slacks, and it was evident that the weight for Capone was now shaved off. Also, surprisingly, gone was any trace of Capone's demeanour, and instead of coming across monosyllabic and rude, he was charming and almost cheerful as he chatted about *The Untouchables*.

'I think it's one of the best movies Brian has done. The thing, though, that I can't sometimes see is ... I can't be objective about ... is how it's going to affect an audience or whatever. Ummmmm, I really ... I can't say what it'll ... aah, I mean it was beautifully done and everything and it holds together and it's ... the thrust of the film is there I can see. I wanted to see it with an audience, and by the time you see this,' he joked to the camera, 'I will have seen it with an audience.'

When he did finally see it with an audience, it was both friend-filled and star-spangled. Paramount used the New York opening of the picture to celebrate its seventy-fifth anniversary in that city, and the lobby of Loew's Astor Plaza Theater was decorated for the event with some of the hottest stars around. Eddie Murphy was there, surrounded by a group of glowering bodyguards, while Sean Penn tried to slink by in sunglasses but was photographed anyway.

When De Niro arrived, he looked questioningly at the gathered photographers as if he really didn't know what all the fuss was about, while co-star Sean Connery, long wise to the ways of the paparazzi, joked with him as they made their way through the crowd.

De Niro's apparent surprise at the press turn-out may have been triggered by a personal reason, as for the first really public time, he was with a date. The woman was model Toukie Smith, a lush black girl whom he'd been seeing for quite a while. Using the old Woody Allen trick of entering and leaving parties and restaurants alone, the couple had never been photographed together, but his close friends had met and known her for some time and he was naturally concerned that the word was getting out and that she'd become the unwilling object of the paparazzi's attention.

After the screening, the guests were limousined over to Roseland for a splashy post-première party, where stars lined up to congratulate De Niro and the other *Untouchables* stars. Matt Dillon was on hand, as were Michael J. Fox, Walter Cronkite, Swoosie Kurtz and Christopher Reeve. Sean Penn zoomed into the party and was in a good mood for a change, talkative, friendly and effusive in his praise to Kevin Costner on his star turn as Eliot Ness. Angela Lansbury, Eric Roberts and Corbin Bernson were also there, as well as co-stars Andy Garcia and Charles Martin Smith.

Almost outshining De Niro and the others was Sean Connery, who'd impressed his peers so much that they were already talking of him as a good bet for an Academy Award nomination. No one could have been more pleased than De Niro, for once again his taking a far-out chance with a part seemed to be successful. And this time he wasn't just getting praise from his fellow actors but from the critics and the public as well.

The preceding day, 3 June 1987, *The Untouchables* had opened, to quote *The Hollywood Reporter*'s Martin A. Grove, 'like gangbusters', grossing a whopping $1.8 million on that first day. Paramount executives began salivating at the mouth as the news trickled in that matinée business on the East Coast was 'going great guns'. Obviously the buzz on *The Untouchables* had been right on the money.

The star trio of Costner, Connery and De Niro proved once again that a good actor needed only a great part to succeed, especially considering that none of their recent pictures had gone anywhere – De Niro's *The Mission* and *Angel Heart*, Connery's *The Name of the Rose* or Costner's *Silverado*. The public response and reviews for the film turned that completely around: Connery received his best notices in years, Kevin Costner was finally acknowledged as a bona fide star, and De Niro experienced an enormous return to mass popularity.

Film-writers all agreed on the superiority of De Palma's direction. Stopping just short of calling him a genius, there was unabashed awe expressed for the way in which he'd told this familiar story, making it seem fresh and spontaneous in the process and a film against which all future gangster films would be judged. *The New York Times* called it a 'big-budget, high-concept and mass-market' tale, 'vulgar, violent, funny and sometimes breathtakingly beautiful and often bloody and outrageous'.

They had a field day dissecting De Niro's Capone, with *Newsweek* leading the pack by asking outright, 'Is De Niro in danger of turning into a latter-day Brando, doing specialty numbers in other people's films?' *The Los Angeles Times*, on the other hand, seemed to appreciate the brevity of his part: 'Lumpish again (you begin to worry for De Niro's heart with all his adding and shedding weight), and icily murderous when he needs to be, De Niro's very brief scenes give the movie its rare and very needed feelings of danger, and its rare shafts of humor.'

The Hollywood Reporter called him '...mesmerizingly intimidating ... when he's on the screen your instinct is to duck and cover', while *New York Magazine* said his was '...a dream character ... his wittiest performance in years'. Writer Chris Chase put the final seal on the comments, though, when she wrote that though De Niro had gained weight and looked jowly, he still '...seems to be having the time of his life behaving so wickedly. When he's finally convicted he acts like one of the Three Stooges, jumping up and down and ranting. It's a fun performance, even though he could probably have done it without the silk drawers.'

As well as making news on the movie pages, De Niro was also making the columns as writers picked up on Toukie Smith. An item in Janet Charlton's *Star People* summed up what was then known: 'Even ROBERT De NIRO, the most secretive man in Hollywood, couldn't keep this news quiet. Close friends say he has become engaged to long-time girlfriend, model TOUKIE SMITH. She was devastated by the AIDS death of her brother, designer Willi Smith, and always appreciated the way De Niro consoled her .... The only person reportedly not delighted with the news is his ex-wife, DIAHNNE ABBOT – she always hoped she and Bob would get back together.'

The relationship had begun long before, in February 1987, a friend says, when De Niro and some pals were hanging out in a bar in New York's trendy SoHo section. Someone in the group recognized the black model and brought her over. She was introduced to De Niro as Doris Smith (her real name), and he was quickly taken with her coltish beauty and straightforward personality. By the end of their first meeting, he'd taken her phone number, and he called the next day to ask her to dinner. Since Doris had decided this darkly not-too-handsome man was a nice guy, she agreed.

At a quiet, New York-darkened restaurant, she relaxed in his company and shortly asked the question that made her seem even more special to him – 'What do you do?'

De Niro replied that he was an actor, and she joked, 'Oh, an actor/model type,' and let it go at that. She didn't recognize him at all, and Bobby was delighted, for he'd often found it difficult to meet women who didn't have some sort of ulterior motive up their sleeve, be it their own career or just being seen with a star. They went out quietly for several months, reportedly, before she realized just exactly who this guy was.

The sister of Willi Smith, a trendy and increasingly popular sportwear designer, she was already an established fashion-show model both for her brother's clothes and for other designers as well. With a ripe figure and an unpretentious face, Toukie radiated an enchanting guilelessness – for example, never worrying about the braces she wore to re-align her buckteeth.

She was very close to her family, and De Niro got along wonderfully with them. When she and her brother had first moved the New York in the late sixties, the two had been inseparable, living in the same West Village apartment building, with Willi in a penthouse and Toukie in an all-red apartment. When his career took off, she was there to share it with him, not to mention help making him into the sensation he became. 'Toukie is my total inspiration,' he enthused. 'She has enough energy to light up the World Trade Center.' When his company did some $39 million worth of business in 1984 alone, he was quick to add that it was due largely to her help, which *Esquire* magazine described as 'a cyclone of dizzy charm'.

When her brother died of AIDS in the spring of 1987, Bobby was by her side, comforting her through the ordeal, and as a special gesture to Toukie and her brother, as well as a larger one to his public, he did a compelling AIDS information spot for commercial television. The public service message stressed how the disease could not be spread through casual contact, contrary to rumours at that time. Serious in close-up and casually powerful, he brought the full power of his screen persona to address these problems and help make it more understandable, though few knew how personal his reason was for doing so. And remember, this was the man who had turned down a fortune from a Japanese beer company and who has always turned down any kind of US commercial offers. This time, though, he was eager to have his face on the small screen, because the cause was so publicly misunderstood and yet so privately important to him.

Among his close circle of friends, Bobby introduced Toukie to Bonnie Timmerman, the casting director for *Miami Vice*, who saw in her just what she was looking for for a forthcoming part.

From its glory days as a Top Ten programme, *Vice* had steadily plummeted to the low forties in the ratings, and the producers were avidly looking for a milestone 'event' to help the show regain some of its initial allure. What they decided on was to get a wife for the 'Sonny Crockett' character, played by Don Johnson. British pop star Sheena Easton, of *For Your Eyes Only* movie-theme fame, was finally picked for the part and, feeling her character needed a confidante and friend, they hired as a recurring guest star Toukie A. Smith.

Toukie's first scene with Don Johnson set the tone of her character as being both caring and understanding. Sheena Easton was introduced in the role of a rock star being threatened by a former record-producer. 'Miami Vice', in the person of Johnson's Crockett, is assigned to protect her, and he shows up, reluctantly, at her door to find Toukie, as Angie, doing the answering. Dressed in a tight orange knitted mini-dress and sporting a dramatically blonded African hairdo, she eyes him up and down as he introduces himself, then pauses and asks, 'You got any credentials other than that pretty face?' It was a startling introduction to De Niro's mystery woman, and her Earth

Mother figure seemed in sharp contrast to Diahnne's crisply classic body and attitude.

In her scenes with Sheena Easton, Toukie exuded a protective warmth and charm while saving a cutting slice of irony for her throwaway lines to Johnson. Large and healthy-looking, she came across as a woman who was quite comfortable with herself and who chose her friends carefully and cautiously. One got the distinct impression that she could give as good as she got, while at the same time being exactly the kind of friend you'd turn to in a pinch.

The episode was heavily publicized, and when it was aired during the ratings sweeps week (when TV networks set their advertising rates by showing their best programmes) it won against *Dallas*, its main competition for viewers' time, which certainly seemed an auspicious beginning for an acting career.

Oddly enough, and probably much to De Niro's relief, Toukie wasn't especially interested in continuing show-business work, as she was perfectly happy with the catering company, Toukie's Taste, that she'd begun and was successfully running. With her own apartments in both New York and Paris, she exhibited yet another side of her independence by maintaining her own addresses and melding the best of her worlds of business and pleasure. She and Bobby spent time together when it was right for both of them. As *Vanity Fair*'s Patricia Bosworth put it, 'They are considered a couple in their small tight circle', and even though De Niro has never formally divorced Diahnne, that doesn't seem to matter to Toukie, and they are expected to remain together.

When *The Untouchables* continued chalking up huge grosses in America, De Niro was amenable to plugging its European success by appearing at the Deauville Film Festival in France, but tried, as usual, to keep a low profile when he wasn't actively working the promotion trail.

One afternoon he was relaxing in the bar of his Deauville hotel when a young man suddenly worked his way across the room, nimbly getting by Bobby's four bodyguards and approaching his table. 'Mr De Niro, Mr De Niro? Don't you remember me? I'm the bellhop who brought you champagne earlier, at your hotel.' De Niro stared up at the youth in silence, not making the connection. Now, without the uniform he'd earlier borrowed just to meet his acting idol, the man introduced himself as Lou Diamond Phillips, the hot young star of *La Bamba*. Always an admirer of good acting, Bobby was suitably impressed. 'That's a good one,' he said with an incredulous smile. 'That was real good, you did it real good.' With his smile broadening, he pulled out some money and stuck it in Diamond's hand. It was an acknowledgement both of the joke and of Diamond's ability to pull it off.

In mid-summer 1987 De Niro accepted a singular, and unprecedented, honour when he accepted an invitation to serve as the head of the main jury at the fifteenth Moscow Film Festival. It was an especially surprising honour in that few, if any, of his films had ever been shown in the Soviet Union. To an opening-night crowd of some 2,500 people,* he quipped that, 'Being an actor, I accepted the role .... It's a great honor and I'm a little nervous.'

By way of introduction, the Russians screened *The Deer Hunter*, which had once been condemned by their movie censors as racist. Afterwards he was asked at a press conference by an elderly Soviet journalist if he felt he had 'compromised his conscience' in acting in the film which had dealt with young Americans of Russian origin participating in the Vietnam War. De Niro was quick to answer, 'No. It was a film against war [and] I certainly do not regret playing in it.' That news conference was made up largely of young Soviet reporters, critics and personnel of the festival – all of whom burst into applause at his reply. These younger Soviets had seen and judged the film according to their own personal principles and had found it good, quite a radical change from a Communist Party cinema handbook which had referred to it as 'a scandalous, racist and militarist film'.

The honesty and acceptance of his hosts prompted De Niro to be more forthcoming about himself, actually sitting down for an interview with a magazine, Germany's *Tempo*. When asked about playing evil, particularly his *Angel Heart* role and then Al Capone in *The Untouchables*, he was blunt about their attractions: 'These characters are not simply bad or evil. They are people living on the edge. I prefer the so-called evil characters because

---

* Other festival guests included Warren Beatty, Federico Fellini, Stanley Kramer, Arthur Penn, Milos Forman, Nastassja Kinski and De Niro's friend and former *1900* co-star Gerard Depardieu.

they're more realistic. Good or only positive characters always tend to be unbelievable and boring. I like to play more rounded characters. A rounded character comes into situations, into trouble, that force them to take decisions. His decisions might not sometimes be the best, but his reactions show the audience they are not alone with their hopes and problems.'

When asked if he had a favourite among his films, he replied, 'Maybe I'll tell you in ten years. I don't like to watch my own movies.' And when the old Travis Bickle/John Hinckley wound was scraped open again, he said, 'There are always people who jump with a towel from the roof because they think they are Superman.'

The interviewer, Wolfgang Wilke, eventually got around to De Niro's physical research into a role and the emotional toll it must take on him. For once, Bobby gave a personal insight into the price of his dedication, telling of an incident that had occurred at the Cannes Film Festival during which he was bloatedly over-weight for his Jake La Motta role. The long-delayed *Once Upon A Time In America* was finally being shown and the stars and director were on hand to give it a personal push, and – 'At the festival, some people said, "Hey, there are Sergio Leone and Robert Woods. But where is Robert De Niro?" I was standing beside them.'

As for his current success as Al Capone, Bobby finished both that subject and that phase of his career by telling how he'd watched the films about Capone's life, looked at all the pictures and digested it all, and then had done the part '...intuitively. Everybody knows Al Capone was a robust, massive character. So I had to gain weight. I could have worn a bodysuit, but what would I have done with my face? So I did the weight thing although I didn't want to and, I promise you, I never will do it again.'

Finally Wilke got to the question that many people were asking: why would America's most reclusive movie star choose to surface in Moscow of all places? 'I went to Moscow to see some movies I never would have seen at home. And I have always felt threatened by the fact that the United States and the Soviet Union are hostile toward each other. However, there are some similari-ties in both countries. We need more mutual information. Movies and personal contacts can help this understanding.'

This interview by a German magazine ironically brought De

Niro face to face with the fact that Vietnam was still a subject of great importance to millions. The recent screen success of *Platoon* had proved that, as had the Soviet reception of *The Deer Hunter*.

While at the Moscow Festival, De Niro had met director David Jones, who'd recently gained fame as the man who made the highly regarded *84 Charing Cross Road*. Now Jones wanted to tackle a drama on the aftermath of Vietnam on the lives of two veterans with personal conflicts still unresolved some fifteen years after the war's end. Called *Jacknife*, he decided it was a movie he wanted to be a part of.

17   *On the Run*

The Moscow Film Festival was both a sobering and an enlightening experience for De Niro, and when he returned home he was anxious to continue his part in changing attitudes towards the Vietnam War. He shortly decided to do the *Jacknife* picture, which was to be, in its theme, a continuation of the Vietnam experience, and he also agreed to take part in *Dear America: Letters Home From Vietnam*. *Dear America* was, initially, a television project, and many other stars, from Robin Williams, Tom Berenger and Martin Sheen to Kathleen Turner and Ellen Burstyn, agreed to contribute their vocal talents by reading actual Vietnam letters over film footage of the war.*

Before *Jacknife*, though, De Niro was offered a complete change of pace with the chance to be funny and make a lot of money at the same time. For a salary reported to be $5 million (some say $6 million), he decided to do a comedy, and since *The Untouchables* had ended up the number five top-grossing picture of 1987 at $76.2 million,† he was in a position to do just about anything he wanted.

De Niro's refreshed fame and more outgoing attitude caused at least one friend to test it, with hilarious results. Sean Penn had been a close friend for several years, and he'd obviously been playing close attention, if not to De Niro's sage advice on celebrity, certainly to the way he said it.

The young actor hosted *Saturday Night Live* just weeks after serving a short gaol term for various assault charges on frantic fans and the press. Anxious to resuscitate an image that had

---

* *Dear America* went on to win a Television Emmy and was scheduled for theatrical release late in 1988.

† The four films ahead of his were *Beverly Hills Cop II* at a smashing $153.6, *Platoon* with $137.9, *Fatal Attraction* $123.5 and *The Golden Child* with $79.8 million.

been badly mauled in the media, Penn was in almost every skit of the ninety-minute comedy show, including one wickedly funny scene in which he impersonated De Niro meeting his agent in a trendy nightclub. (At the height of the club mania, the accent was more and more on private places where celebrities could relax – this mythical club was called The Teeny Café and seated only five people!) Wearing a short, almost punk-styled dark wig (much like De Niro's in real life and as he appeared in *Falling in Love*) Penn produced extraordinary facial movements typical of De Niro grimaces, the tossing of the chin and the rapid repetition of the same question with almost choreographed body movements.

The storyline of the skit was a power meeting to discuss the actor's new movie. We see the agent trying to tell his jittery client that there definitely is a new deal and that all's well, but the star, Bobby, is finding it hard to believe – even though he's been in serious 'training' for it. 'You see my back? ... You see my back?' he questions the agent. 'I had two vertebrae taken out to make me shorter for this movie.' It was not only extremely funny but also testified to Penn's friendship, as only a very close friend could get away with this kind of national television carrying-on.

Things became funnier in print when it was announced that De Niro was being sought for a live action feature of *Peter Pan*. The PPP, or '*Peter Pan* Project', had been making the Hollywood rounds for some time, and always with major names attached to it. At one point, Steven Spielberg was to direct a musical version with Michael Jackson as the boy who never grows up, but, as Spielberg got busier and Michael got older, the project became merely a gossip-column filler. Just after Christmas, though, it took on an air of reality, when Weintraub Entertainment announced it would begin filming in the spring of 1988.

Jerry Weintraub, the husband of sixties hit-maker Jane Morgan, had become one of Hollywood's most successful producers with *The Karate Kid* and could well afford to hire any actor of his choice for the variety of roles available. After all the publicity of Jackson's playing the title role had lived and died in print, he decided to concentrate on the other major parts, especially that of Captain Hook.

Starting the buzz on it early (his organization said filming was to begin the following spring at London's Shepperton Studios), he leaked his 'shortlist' of possible Captain Hooks. Dustin Hoffman was on it somewhere but, said an inside source to the *Los Angeles Times*, 'First is Jack Nicholson – can you imagine what he'd do with a black eye-patch and a hook arm? Next is Mel Gibson – who'd certainly bring something special to the role, but I'm not sure what, exactly. Next is Robert de Niro – who'd probably cut off his arm if he got the role.' Coming, as it did, just shortly after De Niro had stated that his days of making silly putty of his body were over – and after Sean Penn had made a national joke of it, the casting idea became nothing more than an attention-getting, if intriguing column-filler.

Instead, De Niro went to Hollywood to be funny in Universal's *Midnight Run*, and since he'd mentioned in his Moscow interview with Wolfgang Wilke that at this stage in his life 'I only go to Los Angeles when I am paid for it', whether it was for $5 million or $6 million, his fee was obviously enough to get him on the plane.

While he was there, his old friend and Off-Broadway co-star Sally Kirkland became a Best Actress nominee for an Academy Award for *Anna*, and he showed up at publicist Dale Olson's house for a party in her honour, spreading his superstar arms around her for maximum newspaper exposure. Sally had laboured in the actors' vineyard for twenty-five years, and this role was the closest she'd ever got to real stardom. De Niro was there to wish her luck, along with Buck Henry, Robert Blake and Ed Begley Jr. Though she went on to win the Best Actress award from the Los Angeles Critics' Association and the foreign press's Golden Globe, her Oscar race proved to be futile. She did learn who her friends were, though, and perhaps that was almost as important.

Diahnne Abbott was in town about that same time to play a featured part in an episode of television's *Crime Story* series but stayed only long enough to film it. As for De Niro, without an LA home base, he eschewed the familiar comforts of the Château Marmont Hotel in favour of the de-luxe Europeanized version served up at the Bel-Age, just a few blocks further up the Sunset Strip. When the American-Soviet Film Initiative held a fund-raiser in honour of director Elem Klimov, who'd fought against censorship in the Soviet film industry, he had only to come downstairs to join the party.

It was a 'Welcome to Hollywood' party for Klimov and

attracted the likes of director Norman Jewison, Christopher Walken (who was also staying at the Bel-Age) and Dolph Lundgren of *Rocky IV* fame. Dubbed by the *Herald-Examiner* 'Glasnost for Daze', also among the well-wishers was musician Quincy Jones, whose fifty-fifth birthday party had been on De Niro's social agenda just the week before. On that night, though, he seemed bent on improving relations with such Hollywood heavyweights as Barbra Streisand, Don Johnson and Whoopi Goldberg.

At the Klimov party, the wife of Universal's president, Sid Sheinberg, sometime actress Lorraine Gary, chipped away at Glasnost when the caviare ran out: 'That's what they mean by Russian food – you wait in line, and then there isn't any.'

Meanwhile, over at her husband's studio, director Martin Brest was trying to put together the perfect cast for *Midnight Run*. Brest, who'd made a fortune for Paramount two years before with the hugely successful *Beverly Hills Cop*, knew that having De Niro as his star was both a *coup* and a challenge. He later told writer Stephen Farber, 'De Niro is so strong and is such a unique flavor, so to speak .... He's like a weird type of wine that doesn't go with oysters, doesn't go with cheese, doesn't go with spaghetti and clam sauce. I found it very difficult to find a match for him.'

After auditioning a number of actors, Brest concluded that Charles Grodin was the best actor around who could 'synergize with De Niro' as the mob accountant on-the-lam whom De Niro, as a bounty-hunter, is hired to transport across the country. When Brest first had this idea, the film was at Paramount but his backers there were adamant against Grodin because he hadn't had a hit picture in some time – certainly not his most recent, the ill-fated *Ishtar*. They suggested Robin Williams and when he wasn't available urged Brest to rewrite the part for a woman and cast either Cher or Bette Midler. He couldn't agree, they dropped the project and he took it to Universal, where the executives agreed with him and Grodin was signed. Brest was delighted and, as he'd known all along, 'I saw the two of them together, and there was a chemistry.'

Brest concocted the storyline with writer George Gallo, with both working to make the script into an action picture that was funny and touching as well. The formula was a simple one, with De Niro as Jack Walsh, a scruffy ex-cop-turned-bounty-hunter, whose job is to find the missing accountant and bring him back to Los Angeles. He locates him in New York but when, at the airport, the accountant expresses his fear of flying, they have to find other means of travelling, and the adventure is on. Based on an idea of Gallo's, who'd once had a policeman friend caught in a similar situation, this was the springboard for *Midnight Run*.

It was a project that required lots of travelling, and while Brest was off scouting locations in New York, Chicago, Phoenix (Arizona), Las Vegas and New Zealand, De Niro attempted to locate a real-life bounty-hunter for some pointers. He found one too, named Marvin Badler, and the man freely gave the star some tips of his often-dangerous trade. De Niro learned so much, in fact, that Badler was signed on as an 'adviser' on the picture, with his input adding authenticity to several scenes, not to mention costuming. 'De Niro even wears a leather motorcycle jacket like mine in the film,' he later enthused to a reporter.

One of the most difficult aspects of preparing for *Run* was the fact that Bobby would be looking just like himself on screen for the first time since the unsuccessful *Falling in Love* – there would be no layers of extra fat, thinned hairlines or outrageous accents to disguise him. 'To be able to be oneself straight on is hard,' he later observed. 'Actors always feel that they have to do something. If they're not doing anything they're not doing enough. But the fact that they're doing nothing is maybe all they have to do ... [but] you never feel fully satisfied. I'm always waiting to feel fully satisfied.'

At least he had that in common with his character, as Jack Walsh is not satisfied either but a man who's been forced to settle. After quitting the police department for not taking Mafia bribes, he has turned to the seamy life of a bounty-hunter. Offered $100,000 to find the missing Grodin, he takes the job eagerly, seeing the money as a way out.

Grodin's character, Jonathon Mardukas, is a mild-mannered, basically decent guy who's hardly the criminal type. As an accountant for a large company, he's amazed when he finds that it's a front for the Mob. To even the score, he carefully doctors the books until he's embezzled some $15 million from his boss (played by Dennis Farina) and then proceeds to dole it out to charity. After jumping bail, Mardukas gleefully bombards Farina with postcards telling how he's dispersing *his* money, an act that quickly sets the Mob on his trail, as well as Jack Walsh, the FBI *and* a rival bounty-hunter out to grab Walsh's score.

Since they can't fly, the two men start out on a cross-country odyssey that eventually involves train trips, hitchhiking, a shoot-out at the Chicago bus terminal, riding the rails in a boxcar and a helicopter attack from the pursuing gangsters. All the while the pair are feuding with each other as Grodin schemes to escape. He uses the plea that he embezzled only in order to combat the Mob, which strikes a sympathetic chord with Walsh, and the two eventually end up on the same side.

When he was asked what he thought about the script, De Niro replied that it was a good blend of reality and comedy '… and yet it wasn't artificial'. As for his character being pretty much of a normal guy, though, he disagreed, seeking out the loopholes that would make sense to him as an actor. 'I don't think he's normal. I mean, who's normal once you really get to know them? People have their own problems, and life's very complicated.' He did grudgingly admit that, 'He might have been more normal than Travis [Bickle] or some of the other characters [I've played].

As the director, Brest had his hands full juggling the mechanics of this cross-country, ten-city moviemaking machine, and at times the pressure proved intense. That showed itself shortly when, five weeks into the four-month-long shoot, his camera crew, assistant director and several other key personnel quit. Someone who worked on the film told *LA Times* writer Leonard Klady that it was due to a combination of the rigorous pace and a lack of chemistry between Brest and his crew. Said Brest later, 'Generally my instincts about who I'm compatible with are pretty good. This time, I made a mistake.'

It was also obvious that he was interested in getting the most from his two stars, working them six days a week, including rehearsals, sailing through lunch hours and the Thanksgiving holiday in the process. Both De Niro and Grodin appreciated Brest's willingness to work overtime for the good of the film, with Charles adding, 'Marty wants you to work harder, and because he's giving his all, you want to do your best.' Later he added, 'It was a lot of fun, and while we shot the exact script as written, we'd then redo a scene here and there and improvise it – remember the scene in the bus where we're almost becoming friendly? All improvisation.'

Brest had one problem with De Niro, though, when Bobby

wanted to carry this spontaneity over into the stunts. The last scene to be filmed took place in New Zealand, where the cast and crew had gone to find warm rapids water. (It was winter in the US and no suitable place was much above freezing.) De Niro decided that *he* and *not* a double would do a dangerous scene in the water, after his character is chased into the river by the pursuing gangsters. He had to hang on to a rock for dear life as the rapids pounded his body, and Brest recalled, 'I was terrified. It was above an area where not even whitewater experts will go. Had he just slipped, that would have been it.' While Brest felt it was 'debatable' whether the stunt was worth the risk to his star, De Niro did it anyway.

But there was a reason for De Niro's insistence, said Brest. 'His character takes himself so seriously, it's funny. For that to work, the actor has to make the character live and breathe in a very powerful way.'

De Niro was barely back home and unpacked when *Jacknife* got the green light and he was back at work. With his name behind it, the production had been set up quickly. His co-star as the other Vietnam veteran was Ed Harris, an extremely well-regarded actor, though far from being a star of De Niro's stature. Harris' rough-hewn looks and small, muscular body had been used to advantage in a number of successful pictures, particularly as Jessica Lange's husband in her Oscar-nominated biography of singer Patsy Cline, *Sweet Dreams*.

Another advantage to the film was that De Niro was so impressed with it that he was taking only $1.2 million in salary – a huge cut from his *Midnight Run* paycheque. When this was reported, the buzz was that he'd really turned down Penny Marshall and her film, *Big*, because the producers had offered him only $3 million for the part and he wanted $6 million, because he'd heard that that was how much Warren Beatty gets per film. Since De Niro's career decisions have never been made on the basis of salary alone, it made a good, if most unlikely story. His *Jacknife* salary makes it all the more improbable.

Described as the story of two veterans who meet again many years after the war with an unresolved conflict to resolve and 'with a lot of humor thrown into the situation', the film will only increase De Niro's growing image as a symbol of the war and its fighters.

In fact, during the making of *Jacknife*, another incident

happened to cement this viewpoint. It came to light during the publicizing of the television movie *To Heal a Nation*. The film was based on a book of the same name by Vietnam-veteran Jan Scruggs, the man who initiated the move to have the Vietnam Memorial built in Washington DC – a wall of black marble inscribed with the names of the war dead. In an interview Scruggs retold his tale of fighting the opposition to the memorial and how it had all begun. One night in 1979, he and his wife went to the movies, and what they saw was *The Deer Hunter*. It made him relive his own experiences, and he walked out of the theatre emotionally frustrated because he couldn't remember the names of many of the men he'd fought beside and seen die. It was a mind-opening experience, and he determined that a memorial would be the best way of perpetuating their memory. Though many politicians and some war veterans opposed the idea, Scruggs eventually saw his dream realized when the rambling wall of heroes' names was erected in 1984. For him it was the end of nightmares and a beginning of a time of peace and control. For De Niro it was a sign that his work had been not only appreciated but understood, and not just by the average moviegoer but by the survivors of the war itself.

As soon as *Jacknife* finished shooting in Montreal in early July, De Niro began the chore of selling *Midnight Run*, beginning a publicity schedule which included a few taped television talk-show appearances. When *The Untouchables* had opened the previous year, he'd been advised that, with movie competition as rough as it was, he'd be expected to participate in doing publicity. Though it had been only the one show with De Palma, film backers took it as a sign that the public wanted to see the real De Niro as well as his film characters.

Naturally, when *Midnight Run* was about to open, they wanted more, especially since the film was vying for ticket sales in a market-place that included Clint Eastwood's latest Dirty Harry outing, *The Dead Pool*, Eddie Murphy's *Coming to America* and the baseball hit *Bull Durham*. It also faced the competition of another action adventure, the highly touted *Die Hard*, whose star, Bruce Willis, had been making the talk-show rounds for weeks. Though the pictures weren't really anything alike, moviegoers might not know that just by star and title, so it was necessary to get the word out that *Midnight Run* offered comic surprises along with the thrills.

Universal decided the best way to handle it was to set Bobby up in New York hotel ballroom and let the interviewers bring their cameras to him, a technique similar to that used by Beatty and Hoffman for *Ishtar* the year before. By having him occasionally slip into a fresh shirt, it would photograph as if each interviewer was getting an exclusive shot at him. All theatrics, but surprisingly pleasurable ones for the reclusive actor as, watching them, you get a real sense that he's enjoying himself.

Nature helped him take some interviewers even further by surprise for, upon meeting the God of Acting in the flesh, they heard huge claps of thunder from a raging storm outside, causing one publicist to quip, 'These sound effects cost millions!'

Everyone else was interviewed too, and everyone talked. John Ashton, who played the rival bounty-hunter, recalled De Niro's sense of humour. When they were shooting for several days in a tiny Arizona town, the only place to hang out was the local Safeway supermarket. One morning, when a crew member asked Ashton what he'd done the night before, he replied, 'I went to the Safeway.' Bobby looked up at this and replied, 'Really? What aisle were you in?'

Martin Brest confessed that he was initially in total awe of De Niro – 'He's been my idol for fifteen years' – and wasn't disappointed with his star in the least, in fact greatly appreciating what Grodin called his 'fiendish dedication'. Brest told the LA *Herald-Examiner* that, 'I like to do a lot of takes .... Take that scene where De Niro's credit card is canceled. We did 13 or 14 takes of that scene. And you know I kept thinking – I really should do this sometime – get every take of that scene printed up. That would give you a great example of how a scene evolves.' Was this a director who could possibly disappoint De Niro? Hardly.

When the reviews began appearing, each one seemed better than the last. Called the movies' new *Odd Couple* and 'a Laurel and Hardy on the run', the teaming of Grodin and De Niro was widely praised as near comic genius. *Herald Examiner* critic Peter Rainer said they played so well together, 'It's as if they had spent their entire careers warming up for this partnership.' De Niro felt this too, telling Gene Shalit how, 'Chuck is a very different actor from me, very reserved, very close with his emotions .... It worked very well for us ... and he was always willing to try something new.'

De Niro's comic abilities left writers grabbing for new adjectives, his reality in becoming the rent-a-thug ex-cop as impressive as any of the transformations he'd done before in front of a camera. Michael Wilmington of the *Los Angeles Times* asked, 'When all good actors die and go to heaven, do they get to be Robert De Niro? In the last decade he's become a real symbol of excellence, somewhat as Brando was in his day, or Spencer Tracy in his. And De Niro deserves it; he's a genius ....'

When *Midnight Run* was screened at New York's Sutton Theater, Bobby displayed a new sense of personal cool when he jumped out of the studio limousine to greet the crowd of photographers surrounding the theatre. He was fast becoming a practised hand at it, unlike his friend Sean Penn, who slunk in with his usual anti-social demeanour. Liza Minelli, though still reeling from the box-office failure of her *Arthur 2 – On the Rocks*, giggled and smiled for the flashbulbs. Her career had lasted long enough for her also to realize that one bad picture wouldn't bury it.

At the post-screening party held downtown at the Greene Street Café, Robert De Niro Senior was a surprise guest. With his white Borsolino hat planted firmly on his head and his cotton suit rumpled from the latest New York heatwave, he looked uncannily like an older version of his namesake son. The party was filled with other names – Brooke Shields, Ralph Macchio, Debbie Harry – and keeping back out of the flashbulbs' way was, as usual, Toukie Smith, there to share in the triumph if not the coverage.

Bobby De Niro's private world is tightly knit. His friends keep their silence – or lose his friendship – while his enemies are surprisingly few. Investments, money and career moves are overseen by a trusted few, and he's now secure enough with this celebrity to rely on nothing more than a pair of glasses to feel anonymous.

The press and the tabloids use his name regularly for publicity – as with the romantic linking of it recently with singer Whitney Houston, an item shortly followed by the 'news' that the pair would co-star in a remake of the old Doris Day musical *Love Me or Leave Me* – and the stories are lively copy. He's always good for a Brando-like item, such as the one where he'd recently paid

$5 million for his own South Pacific island – after refusing Brando's, for sale at $10 million, because it was too much of a tourist attraction. By now he realized that all of that goes with the territory of stardom and that, while he may originally have wanted nothing more than to be a working actor, he's now stuck with the label of Supershy Superstar.

One rumour that did prove true was his making a film with Jane Fonda, and sharing top-billing for the first time in years. Jane Fonda set off a barrage of protest from Vietnam veterans when she first tried to get permission to film in Massachusetts. Her old image as 'Hanoi Jane', a label she won as an anti-war activist and by her visit to Hanoi at the height of the war in 1972, came back to haunt her, causing such an outcry that she had to go on Barbara Walters' television show and apologize to the country.

De Niro's name came into the project only once this dust had settled, with the original title, *Union Street*, switched to *Stanley and Iris* to negate the bad publicity *Union Street* had garnered. With director Martin Ritt at the helm, De Niro began work on it just as *Midnight Run* was becoming a success at the box-office.

It was described as a tender comedy love story. The pair portray workers in a cake factory from which De Niro's Stanley is fired when it becomes known he's illiterate. Jane Fonda's Iris teaches him to read, and a romance develops from there. Retitled yet again, it's now called *Letters*, but the box-office fate of a Vietnam icon and Hanoi Jane remains to be seen.

Perhaps this time a romantic comedy will do well for De Niro, despite questionable casting. The only thing he really looks for in the beginning is the word. When asked what he looks for in a script, he said, 'Everything is different; you just can't tell. The script could have something that I've never even thought of, that I like, and I say "Oh this is interesting, and I'd like to do it." It could just be anything from anywhere, and that's part of the excitement about it.'

There are new worlds for De Niro to conquer, and one he's persistently said to be intrigued by is directing, in particular a movie based on Phillip Carlo's novel *Stolen Flowers*. In it he would star as a private eye tracking down the abductors of a nine-year-old girl who's been sold into prostitution. It's a fascinating thought for many as to what De Niro the director might bring to De Niro the actor.

Another collaboration with Martin Scorsese might also be in the offing. 'Bob and I are trying to find a common link again,' the director has said. 'After *The King of Comedy* we decided to go our separate ways. We needed to work with other people. We had worked so intensely for so many years. Now we're actively looking for something – no, I can't tell you what, but it's going to be different from anything we did before. We're older now, we're interested in different stuff, and it's not so much the material but how we connect with it emotionally.'

Connecting emotionally seems to be the key to both De Niro's career and his private life, and what people might think of that approach doesn't matter to him one bit. On screen he's interpreted men who've been forced to handle life with what they've been dealt, be it the killing anti-sociality of Travis Bickle, the bloody rage of Jake La Motta or the sidetracked tenacity of Rupert Pupkin. In each case he's used his probing talent to strip away the layers and to make even these unregenerate people somehow understandable, if not acceptable.

As he sifts through the endless piles of scripts that flood his Manhattan loft, cautiously shielded by assistants, friends and family, perhaps the image that's really the closest to him is the singleminded dedication that was the hallmark of Monroe Stahr, *The Last Tycoon*, who, after going through an elaborately mysterious charade, suddenly stops. When someone anxiously enquires, 'What's next?', he smiles slowly and innocently into the camera's eye. 'I don't know. I was just making pictures.'

Filmography

The Wedding Party (Ondine Productions, 1966)
Directors: Cynthia Munroe, Brian De Palma, Wilford Leach
Producers: Cynthia Munroe, Brian De Palma, Wilford Leach
Screenplay: Cynthia Munroe, Brian De Palma, Wilford Leach
Director of Photography: Peter Powell
Film Editors: Cynthia Munroe, Brian De Palma, Wilford Leach
Music: John McDowell
Running Time: 88 minutes

Josephine Fish	Jill Clayburgh
Charlie	Charles Pfluger
Mrs Fish	Valda Setterfield
Phoebe	Jennifer Salt
Mr Fish	Raymond McNally
Reverend Oldfield	John Braswell
Celeste	Judy Thomas
Nanny	Sue Ann Converse
Baker	John Quinn
Cecil	Robert De Niro
Alistair	William Finley

This black-and-white production details the anxieties, foibles and fantasies of a group of people gathered in a remote location for a wedding. Centring on the groom and his two best friends, it's a surprising comedy outing, especially in light of its meagre budget and novice cast.

Greetings (West End Films, 1968)
Director: Brian De Palma
Producers: Charles Hirsch
Screenplay: Charles Hirsch and Brian De Palma

Director of Photography: Robert Fiore
Film Editor: Brian De Palma
Music: The Children of Paradise
Running Time: 88 minutes

Paul Shaw	Jonathon Warden
Jon Rubin	Robert De Niro
Lloyd Clay	Gerrit Graham
Marina	Megan McCormick
Secretary	Ashley Oliver
Divorcée	Cynthia Pelts
Linda	Ruth Alda
Pornography-seller	Allen Garfield
Photographer	Ros Kelly
Himself	Lyndon B. Johnson

One of the most successful independent films of the late sixties, this cheaply shot story tells the varied tales of three young men trying to evade the draft for the Vietnam war. De Niro plays an obsessive sexual voyeur who pretends to be a member of a secret underground military group to avoid induction into the regular army.

Sam's Song, also *The Swap* (1969; released as *The Swap* by the Cannon Group, 1983)
Director: John Shade
Producer: Christopher C. Dewey
Screenplay: John C. Broderick
Director of Photography: Alex Phillips
Film Editor: Arline Garson
Running time: 90 minutes

Vito	Anthony Charnoto
Sammy	Robert De Niro

with Jennifer Warren, Lisa Blount, Sybil Danning, Jerry Mickey

A major De Niro career curiosity since he's killed off early on and his brother spends the rest of the film trying to find out why. When De Niro had established himself as a bona-fide superstar, this cheap thriller was dusted off, and unused footage of the actor was haphazardly inserted to beef up his on-screen time. This, plus a new title, deceived few people into thinking it was a new work as had obviously been intended.

Bloody Mama (American International, 1969)
Director: Roger Corman
Producer: Roger Corman
Executive Producers: Samuel Z. Arkoff, James H. Nicholson
Screenplay: Robert Thom, Don Peters
Director of Photography: John Alonzo
Film Editor: Eve Newman
Music: Don Randi
Running Time: 90 minutes

Kate 'Ma' Barker	Shelley Winters
Sam Adams Pendlebury	Pat Hingle
Herman Barker	Don Stroud
Mona Gibson	Diane Varsi
Kevin Dirkman	Bruce Dern
Arthur Barker	Clint Kimbrough
Lloyd Barker	Robert De Niro
Fred Barker	Robert Walden
George Barker	Alex Nicol
Dr Roth	Michael Fox
Moses	Scatman Crothers

'Ma' Barker and her murderous brood hit the screen in this slam-bang free-for-all. As 'Ma's' loony son Lloyd, De Niro exercised early aspects of the manic screen personality yet to evolve. Though admittedly a popcorn-seller, this film did give De Niro his widest screen exposure to date.

Hi. Mom! (West End Films, 1969)
Director: Brian De Palma
Producer: Charles Hirsch
Screenplay: Brian De Palma from a story by Charles Hirsch and Brian De Palma
Director of Photography: Robert Elfstrom
Film Editor: Paul Hirsch
Music: Eric Kas
Running time: 86 minutes

Jon Rubin	Robert De Niro
Judy Bishop	Jennifer Salt
Jeannie Mitchell	Lara Parker
Gerrit Wood	Gerrit Graham
Playboy	Nelson Pelts
Superintendent	Charles Durnham
Joe Banner	Allen Garfield
Pervert	Abraham Goren

This sequel to *Greetings* finds our hero, Jon Rubin (De Niro), home from the Vietnam War and eager to return to his avocation as a voyeur. This time he tries to go professional, however, filming the lives of four apartments' occupants. This leads to more active photography, concentrating on the raising of 'black consciousness' in America. After his efforts are violently rejected by those concerned, Rubin returns to an unsatisfactory home life – which he shortly blows up via his demolition expertise learned in the war. De Niro's first top-billed performance, it does give the viewer a flash of the screen persona yet to evolve.

Jennifer On My Mind (Joseph M. Schenck Enterprises, 1971)
Director: Noel Black
Producer: Bernard Schwartz
Screenplay: Erich Segal, based on the novel *Heir* by Roger L. Simon
Director of Photography: Andrew Laszlo
Film Editor: Jack Wheeler
Music: Stephen J. Lawrence
Running time: 90 minutes

Marcus Rottner	Michael Brandon
Jennifer Da Silva	Tippy Walker
Max Rottner	Lou Gilbert
Sigmund Ornstein	Steve Vinovich
Sergei	Peter Boners
Selma	Renee Taylor
Sam	Chuck McCann
Lerry Dolci	Bruce Kornbluth
Nanki	Barry Bostwick
Hanki	Jeff Conaway

Mardigan	Robert De Niro
Gondolier	Erich Segal

Michael Brandon and Tippy Walker were the best things about this dark and gloomy drama of drug-abuse among the wealthy. Writer Erich Segal appears as a Venetian gondolier, with De Niro appearing briefly – and prophetically – as a gypsy taxi-driver.

Born to Win (United Artists, 1971)
Director: Ivan Passer
Producer: Philip Langner
Screenplay: David Scott Milton
Directors of Photography: Jack Priestly, Richard Kratina
Film Editor: Ralph Rosenbaum
Music: William S. Fisher
Running time: 90 minutes

Jay Jay	George Segal
Parm	Karen Black
Billy Dynamite	Jay Fletcher
The Geek	Hector Elizondo
Marlene	Marcia Jean Kurtz
Stanley	Irving Selbst
Danny	Robert De Niro
Veronica	Paula Prentiss
Cashier	Sylvia Syms

A self-indulgent black comedy about heroin-addiction, *Born to Win* had the much more appropriate shooting title of *Scraping Bottom*. Despite an excellent cast, it was little seen and little missed.

The Gang That Couldn't Shoot Straight (MGM-Chartoff/Winkler, 1971)
Director: James Goldstone
Producers: Irwin Winkler, Robert Chartoff
Screenplay: Waldo Salt, based on the novel by Jimmy Breslin
Director of Photography: Owen Roizman
Film Editor: Edward A. Biery
Music: Dave Grusin

Running time: 96 minutes

'Kid Sally' Palumbo	Jerry Ohrbach
Angela	Leigh Taylor-Young
Big Momma	Jo Van Fleet
Baccala	Lionel Stander
Mario	Robert De Niro
Big Jelly	Irving Selbst
Beppo	Herve Villechaize
Ezmo	Joe Santos
Tony the Indian	Carmine Caridi
Water Buffalo	Frank Campanella
De Lauria	Harry Basch
TV commentator	Sander Vanocur

This well-intentioned comedy spoof of the gangster film genre quickly misfires into a string of bad jokes and overbroad performances. De Niro's loopy character, however, manages not only to join the fun but to make his scenes *funny*, garnering him, in the process, some very good reviews. The film also showcases Jo Van Fleet in a rare comic turn as a Mafia grandmother.

Bang the Drum Slowly (ANJA Films, 1973)
Director: John Hancock
Producer: Maurice and Lois Rosenfield
Screenplay: Mark Harris
Director of Photography: Richard Shore
Film Editor: Richard Marks
Music: Stephen Lawrence
Running time: 98 minutes

Bruce Pearson	Robert De Niro
Henry Wiggen	Michael Moriarty
Dutch Schnell	Vincent Gardenia
Joe Jaros	Phil Foster
Katie	Ann Wedgeworth
Mr Pearson	Patrick McVey
Holly Wiggen	Heather MaCrae
Tootsie	Selma Diamond
Team owners	Barbara Babcock, Maurice Rosenfield
Piney Woods	Tom Ligon

| Aleck Olson | Nicolas Surovy |
| Horse | Danny Aiello |

Marking De Niro's first film in a starring role, *Bang the Drum*, if nothing else, represents his 'major film' example of self-submergence into character. As the bumbling tobacco-chewing baseball catcher dying of cancer, De Niro injected every dimension of the pathos, spirit and failing energy the part required. His superb co-stars added all the precisely right emotions and reactions. The result is a timeless study of a man in agony and the friends who suffer with him.

Mean Streets (Taplin-Perry-Scorsese, 1973)
Director: Martin Scorsese
Producer: Jonathon T. Taplin
Screenplay: Martin Scorsese, Mardik Martin, based on Scorsese's story
Director of Photography: Kent Wakeford
Film Editor: Sid Levin
Music: Various Artists
Running time: 110 minutes

Johnny Boy	Robert De Niro
Charlie	Harvey Keitel
Tony	David Proval
Teresa	Amy Robinson
Michael	Richard Romanus
Giovanni	Cesare Danova
Mario	Vic Argo
Assassin	Robert Carradine
Diane	Jeannie Bell
Cop	D'Mitch Davis
Drunk in bar	David Carradine
Car gunman	Martin Scorsese

Abrasively violent and well received by critics, *Mean Streets* was a box-office dud. As the compulsively violent gangster, Johnny Boy, De Niro is stunningly effective and thoroughly believable. A perfect launch-pad for what was quickly to follow – the title role in *The Godfather Part II*.

The Godfather Part II (Paramount Pictures, 1974)
Director: Francis Ford Coppola
Producer: Francis Ford Coppola
Screenplay: Francis Ford Coppola, Mario Puzo, based on *The Godfather* by Mario Puzo
Director of Photography: Gordon Willis
Film Editors: Peter Zinner, Barry Malkin, Richard Marks
Music: Nino Rota, conducted by Carmine Coppola
Running time: 200 minutes

Michael	Al Pacino
Tom Hagen	Robert Duvall
Kay	Diane Keaton
Vito Corleone	Robert De Niro
Fredo Corleone	John Cazale
Connie Corleone	Talia Shire
Hyman Roth	Lee Strasberg
Frankie Pentangeli	Michael Gazzo
Senator Geary	G.D. Spradlin
Al Neri	Richard Bright
Fanucci	Gaston Moschin
Mama Corleone	Morgana King
Merle Johnson	Troy Donahue
Carlo	Gianni Russo

This continuation of *The Godfather* saga presented De Niro as the young Vito Corleone. Displaying an understated sense of total power and authority, he commanded the screen so effectively that he won the Best Supporting Actor Academy Award – and was finally and truly launched as a major star.

1900 (Novecento) (PEA, 1976)
Director: Bernardo Bertolucci
Producer: Alberto Grimaldi
Screenplay: Bernardo Bertolucci, Franco Arcalli, Giuseppe Bertolucci
Director of Photography: Vittorio Storaro
Film Editor: Franco Arcalli
Music: Ennio Morricone
Running time: 320 minutes but edited down to various lengths for international markets

Alfredo	Robert De Niro
Olmo Dalco	Gerard Depardieu
Ada Fiastri Paulhan	Dominique Sanda
Anita Foschi	Stefania Sandrelli
Attila	Donald Sutherland
Alfredo Berlinghieri	Burt Lancaster
Leo Dalco	Sterling Hayden
Regina	Laura Betti
Signora Pioppi	Alida Valli
Ottavio	Werner Bruhns
Amelia	Ellen Schwiers
Giovanni	Romolo Valli

Italy at the turn of the century is the setting for Bertolucci's gigantic epic, with De Niro and Gerard Depardieu as childhood friends adapting to a world of change and unrest. De Niro's aristocratic 'Alfredo' grows from a life of ease into one of basic reality, with Depardieu his counterpart in change.

Taxi Driver (Columbia Pictures, 1976)
Director: Martin Scorsese
Producers: Michael Phillips, Julia Phillips
Screenplay: Paul Schrader
Director of Photography: Michael Chapman
Film Editor: Marcia Lucas
Music: Bernard Herrmann
Running time: 114 minutes

Travis Bickle	Robert De Niro
Betsy	Cybill Shepherd
Iris	Jodie Foster
Tom	Albert Brooks
Sport	Harvey Keitel
Charles Palantine	Leonard Harris
Wizard	Peter Boyle
Gun salesman	Steven Prince
Taxi passenger	Martin Scorsese
Concession attendant	Diahnne Abbott

A devastating commentary on loneliness and alienation in a big city, *Taxi Driver* became an instant cult classic. Robert De Niro's riveting portrayal of a disorientated veteran who drives a cab at nights because he 'can't sleep' launched one of the catchphrases of the late 1970s – 'You talkin' to me?' Its frank and open street language was a shocker for its time but worked perfectly in the structure of the story of an isolated man.

The Last Tycoon (Paramount Pictures, 1976)
Director: Elia Kazan
Producer: Sam Spiegel
Screenplay: Harold Pinter, from the novel by F. Scott Fitzgerald
Director of Photography: Victor Kemper
Film Editor: Richard Marks
Music: Maurice Jarre
Running time: 124 minutes

Monroe Stahr	Robert De Niro
Rodriguez	Tony Curtis
Pat Brady	Robert Mitchum
Didi	Jeanne Moreau
Brimmer	Jack Nicholson
Boxley	Donald Pleasance
Kathleen Moore	Ingrid Boulting
Fleishacker	Ray Milland
Red Ridingwood	Dana Andrews
Cecilia Brady	Theresa Russell
Wylie	Peter Strauss
Edna	Angelica Huston

In this story based on Fitzgerald's unfinished novel of Hollywood power and glory, De Niro's an Irving Thalberg-type movie mogul who becomes enchanted with a young beauty (Ingrid Boulting) who reminds him of his late wife. De Niro playing the elegant producer is a powerfully effective sight to see – though not many people paid to do so.

New York, New York (Chartoff-Winkler, 1977)
Director: Martin Scorsese
Producers: Irwin Winkler, Robert Chartoff
Screenplay: Earl MacRauch, Mardik Martin, based on a story by MacRauch
Director of Photography: Lazlo Kovacs

Film Editors: Tom Rolf, B. Lovitt, David Ramirez
Musical Director: Ralph Burns with original material by John Kander and Fred Ebb
Running time: 153 minutes

Francine Evans	Liza Minelli
Jimmy Doyle	Robert De Niro
Tony Harwell	Lionel Stander
Paul Wilson	Barry Primus
Bernice	Mary Kay Place
Frankie Harte	Georgie Auld
Nicky	George Memmoli
Palm Club owner	Dick Miller
Horace Morris	Murray Moston
Harlem Club singer	Diahnne Abbott
Cab driver	Nicky Blair
D.J.	Casey Kasem
Hairdresser	Sydney Guilaroff
The girlfriend	Shera Danese

The *Taxi Driver* meets *Lullaby of Broadway* in this most oddball of movie musicals. De Niro's annoyingly obsessive feelings for band singer Liza Minelli make for an uneasy blend of song and stance stirred together by Martin Scorsese.

The Deer Hunter (EMI films, 1978)
Director: Michael Cimino
Producers: Barry Spikings, Michael Deeley, Michael Cimino, John Peverall
Screenplay: Deric Washburn, based on a story by Washburn, Michael Cimino, Louis Garkinkle and Quinn Redeker
Director of Photography: Vilmos Zsigmond
Film Editor: Peter Zinner
Music: Stanley Myers
Running time: 182 minutes

Michael Vronsky	Robert De Niro
Stan	John Cazale
Steven	John Savage
Linda	Meryl Streep
Nick	Christopher Walken

John	George Dzunda
Axel	Chuck Aspegren
Steven's mother	Shirley Stoler
Angela	Rutanya Alda
Julien	Pierre Segui
Axel's girl	Mady Kaplan
Bridesmaid	Amy Wright
Stan's girl	Mary Ann Haenel
Linda's father	Richard Kuss
Bandleader	Joe Grifasi

Director Cimino's three-hour journey into the lives of three young steelworkers who serve in Vietnam remains one of the most poignant anti-war films of all time. Physically and emotionally shocking, it exhausts its audiences in proving its point.

Raging Bull (United Artists, 1980)
Director: Martin Scorsese
Producers: Irwin Winkler, Robert Chartoff
Screenplay: Paul Schrader, Mardik Martin, based on *Raging Bull* by Jake La Motta, Peter Savage and Joseph Carter
Director of Photography: Michael Chapman
Film Editor: Thelma Schoonmaker
Music: Pietro Mascagni
Running time: 129 minutes

Jake La Motta	Robert De Niro
Vickie La Motta	Cathy Moriarty
Joey	Joe Pesci
Salvy	Frank Vincent
Tommy Como	Nicholas Colasanto
Lenore	Theresa Saldana
Patsy	Frank Adonis
Mario	Mario Gallo
Toppy	Frank Topham
Irma	Lori Anne Flax
Guido	Joseph Bono
Dr Pinto	James V. Christy
Comedian	Bernie Allen
Reporter	Bill Mazer

Critics and public alike agreed that De Niro's performance as
boxer Jake La Motta was a knockout deserving of an Academy
Award. They were all proved correct when he went on to win
the Best Actor Oscar.

True Confessions (United Artists, 1981)
Director: Ulu Grosbard
Producers: Irwin Winkler, Robert Chartoff
Screenplay: John Gregory Dunne and Joan Didion, based on
Dunne's novel
Director of Photography: Owen Roizman
Film Editor: Lynzee Klingman
Music: Georges Delerue
Running time: 108 minutes

Des Spellacy	Robert De Niro
Tom Spellacy	Robert Duvall
Seamus Fargo	Burgess Meredith
Jack Amsterdam	Charles Durning
Dan T. Campion	Ed Flanders
Cardinal Danaher	Cyril Cusack
Frank Crotty	Kenneth McMillan
Howard Terkel	Dan Hedeya
Brenda Samuels	Rose Gregorio
Mrs Spellacy	Jeanette Nolan
Whore	Louisa Moritz

Two Irish brothers grow up and go in different directions – one
to become a respected policeman and the other a Catholic priest
(De Niro). When Tom Spellacy finds out his brother, now a
monsignor, is involved with a murderous tycoon, he has to
turn him in. One of De Niro's most subdued and responsible
performances.

The King of Comedy (Embassy International, 1982)
Director: Martin Scorsese
Producer: Arnon Milchan
Screenplay: Paul D. Zimmerman
Director of Photography: Fred Schuler
Film Editor: Thelma Schoonmaker
Music: Robbie Robertson

Running time: 108 minutes

Rupert Pupkin	Robert De Niro
Jerry Langford	Jerry Lewis
Rita	Diahnne Abbott
Masha	Sandra Bernhard
Ed Herlihy	Himself
Stage Door Guard	Whitey Ryan
Band leader	Lou Brown
Chauffeur	Doc Lawless
Young girl	Marta Heflin
Rupert's mother	Catherine Scorsese
Dolores	Cathy Scorsese
Receptionist	Margo Winkler
Cathy Long	Shelley Hack
Dr Joyce Brothers	Herself
Victor Borge	Himself
TV director	Martin Scorsese

This black comedy pits a pathetically obsessed fan (De Niro) against his idol (Jerry Lewis) – and no one comes up the winner except the actors. Lewis and De Niro each gave *tour-de-force* performances which critics raved over and few of the public went to see. A milestone in film comedy nonetheless.

Once Upon A Time In America (Embassy International, 1983)
Director: Sergio Leone
Producer: Arnon Milchan
Screenplay: Sergio Leone, Leonardo Benvenuti Piero DeBernardi, Enrico Medioli, Franco Arcalli, Franco Ferrini
Director of Photography: Tonino Delli Colli
Film Editor: Nino Baragli
Music: Ennio Morricone
Running time: 228 minutes (theatrical American version, 144 minutes)

Noodles	Robert De Niro
Max	James Wood
Deborah	Elizabeth McGovern
Joe	Burt Young
Carol	Tuesday Weld

Frankie	Joe Pesci
Jimmy O'Donnell	Treat Williams
Police Chief	Danny Aiello
Cockeye	William Forsythe
Patsy	James Hayden
Eve	Darlanne Fleugel
Fat Moe	Larry Rapp

In its uncut form (available on video-cassette), *Once Upon A Time ...* is a melancholy masterpiece which traces the lives of five Jewish youngsters and their rise into the dangerous echelons of gangsterism. Unappreciated on its initial release, the uncut version is now considered a classic of the genre. It took director Leone thirteen years to bring it to the screen.

Falling In Love (Paramount Pictures, 1984)
Director: Ulu Grosbard
Producer: Marvin Worth
Screenplay: Michael Cristofer
Director of Photography: Peter Suschitzky
Film Editor: Michael Kahn
Music: Dave Grusin
Running time: 106 minutes

Frank Raftis	Robert De Niro
Molly Gilmore	Meryl Streep
Ann Raftis	Jane Kaczmarek
John Trainer	George Martin
Brian Gilmore	David Clennon
Isabelle	Dianne Wiest
Ed Lasky	Harvey Keitel
Victor Rawlins	Victor Argo
Mike Raftis	Wiley Earl

Falling In Love is De Niro's first attempt at being a main-line matinée lover boy. Unfortunately his repertoire of mixed-up, often near-crazy and often sociopathic screen characters made it almost impossible for moviegoers to accept him as a romantic leading man. Largely a waste of his and Meryl Streep's talent – and a lot of the producer's money.

Brazil (Universal Pictures, 1985)
Director: Terry Gilliam
Producer: Arnon Milchan
Screenplay: Terry Gilliam, Tom Stoppard, Charles McKeown
Director of Photography: Roger Pratt
Film Editor: Julian Doyle
Music: Michael Kamen
Running time: 142 minutes

Sam Lowry	Jonathan Pryce
Harry Tuttle	Robert De Niro
Ida Lowry	Katherine Helmond
Mr Kurtzman	Ian Holm
Spoor	Bob Hoskins
Jack Lint	Michael Palin
Mr Warren	Ian Richardson
Mr Helpmann	Peter Vaughn
Jill Layton	Kim Greist
Dr Jaffe	Jim Broadbent
Mrs Terrain	Barbara Hicks

One of the most controversial films of 1985 because of its length
(and how it should be edited), *Brazil* is also one of the strangest.
Set in an Orwellian future, the picture is dynamic to look at but
surpassingly hard to understand. If its purpose was to predict
the future as being insane and out of control, it succeeded
admirably. One reviewer succinctly summed it up saying, 'The
best part is the theme song.'

The Mission (Warner Brothers, 1986)
Director: Roland Joffe
Producer: Fernando Ghia
Screenplay: Robert Bolt
Director of Photography: Chris Menges
Film Editor: Jim Clark
Music: Ennio Morricone
Running time: 126 minutes

Mendoza	Robert De Niro
Gabriel	Jeremy Irons
Altamirano	Ray McAnally

Carlotta	Cherie Lunghi
Hontar	Ronald Pickup
Ibaye	Monirak Sisowath
Felipe	Aidan Quinn
Fielding	Liam Neeson

This historical epic pits a missionary (Irons) against a mercenary (De Niro) until the latter's religious conversion brings them both to the same side. Set in South America in the mid-eighteenth century, it details the struggles of an honest priest and his followers to end the slave-trading of the Guarani Indians. The film's executive producer called it 'a Clint Eastwood version of *Beckett* – an intellectual theme treated with guts'. De Niro was dashing, humble, contrite and devout in turn but was mostly accused of over-acting.

Angel Heart (Carolco Pictures, 1986)
Director: Alan Parker
Producers: Alan Marshall, Elliot Kastner
Screenplay: Alan Parker, based on William Hjortsberg's novel
Director of Photography: Michael Seresin
Film Editor: Gerry Hambling
Music: Trevor Jones
Running time: 113 minutes

Harry Angel	Mickey Rourke
Louis Cyphre	Robert De Niro
Epiphany Proudfoot	Lisa Bonet
Margaret	Charlotte Rampling
Toots Sweet	Brownie McGhee
Ethan Krusemark	Stocker Fontelieu

A dark and extremely controversial film, *Angel Heart* explores the seamy world of gangsters and voodoo in New Orleans during the mid 1950s. Rourke literally goes to the devil when a mysterious man (De Niro) hires his detecting abilities to locate a long-lost former associate. The brouhaha engendered by the film's explicit sexuality made headlines for weeks until the director cut the offending scene and it was released to a tepid box-office.

The Untouchables (Paramount Pictures, 1987)
Director: Brian De Palma
Producer: Art Linson
Screenplay: David Mamet
Director of Photography: Stephen H. Burum
Film Editor: Jerry Greenberg
Music: Ennio Morricone
Running time: 119 minutes

Eliot Ness	Kevin Costner
Al Capone	Robert De Niro
Jim Malone	Sean Connery
George Stone	Andy Garcia
Oscar Wallace	Charles Martin Smith
Frank Nitti	Billy Drago

'The Untouchables' ride again as the story of the G-men versus the Mob is resurrected in a film often funny, violent, vulgar and hauntingly beautiful. Good Guy Eliot Ness (Costner) confronts the king of the underworld himself, Al Capone (De Niro), in a bloody and outrageous shoot-out which, stylistically, harks back to the days of Eisenstein in its filmic scope and power. De Niro – this time aided by some thirty pounds extra weight – commands the screen in a chillingly acclaimed performance.

Dear America, Letters Home From Vietnam (HBO, 1987)
Director: Bill Couturie
Producers: Bill Couturie, Thomas Bird
Screenwriters: Richard Dewhurst, Bill Couturie
Film Editor: Stephen Stept
Music: Todd Boekelheide and assorted artists
Running time: 132 minutes (also shown in an 85-minute version)

In alphabetical order the actors heard are Tom Berenger, Ellen Burstyn, J. Kenneth Campbell, Richard Chaves, Josh Cruze, Willem Dafoe, Robert De Niro, Brian Dennehy, Kevin Dillon, Robert Downey Jr, Michael J. Fox, Mark Harmon, John Heard, Fred Hirz, Harvey Keitel, Elizabeth McGovern, Judd Nelson, Sean Penn, Randy Quaid, Tom Quill, Eric Roberts, Ray Robertson, Howard Rollins Jr, John Savage, Raphael Sbarge, Martin Sheen, Tucker Smallwood, Roger Steffens, Jim Tracy, Kathleen Turner, Tico Wells and Robin Williams, with the music of such artists as The Band, The Doors, Jimi Hendrix, Elvis

Presley, the Rolling Stones, Sonny and Cher, and Bruce Springsteen.

Utilizing the vocal talents of many stars, authentic letters home from Vietnam soldiers are read over graphic film material of the war amassed from sources including declassified Pentagon archives, NBC News footage and amateur 8 mm film shot by servicemen in the field. A seamless blend of telejournalism highlighted by the music of the times, *Dear America*, according to the *Los Angeles Times*, '...is surely the most authentic of all the recent Vietnam films'. It frankly examines the American experience in that country in the most chillingly realistic of terms. Hauntingly subtitled 'P.S. I hope you hear me this time ...'.

Midnight Run (Universal Pictures release of a City Lights Film, 1988)
Director: Martin Brest
Producer: Martin Brest
Screenwriter: George Gallo
Director of Photography: Donald Thorin
Film Editors: Billy Weber, Chris Lebenzon and Michael Tronick
Music: Danny Elfman
Running time: 123 minutes

Jack Walsh	Robert De Niro
Jonathon Mardukas	Charles Grodin
Alonzo Mosely	Yaphet Kotto
Marvin Dorfler	John Ashton
Jimmy Serrano	Dennis Farina
Eddie Moscone	Joe Pantoliano
Tony Darvo	Richard Foronjy
Joey	Robert Miranda

De Niro plays a bounty-hunter on the trail of a mild-mannered accountant (Charles Grodin) who's made off with some $15 million – only to find out that Grodin's donated it all to charity. De Niro has to return Grodin to the clutches of the mob via a cross-country chase involving other bounty-hunters, angry gangsters and their clutch of incompetent hitmen. Loud, boisterous and enormously funny, the film was critically applauded, with De Niro's sense of comedy (not seen in years) hailed as 'genius'.

Index